MW00654305

"God is preparing His heroes; and when opportunity comes,
He can fit them into their places in a moment,
and the world will wonder where they came from."

—A.B. Simpson

A WARRIOR'S PRAYERBOOK

FOR SPIRITUAL WARFARE

Be strong and courageous.
Do not be frightened, and do not be dismayed,
for the Lord your God is with you wherever you go.

JOSHUA 1:9

PRAYERS · SCRIPTURES · THOUGHTS

Compiled by

Kathryn McBride

Letcetera
PUBLISHING
CHICAGO

ACKNOWLEDGMENTS

Special thanks to my friend and mentor Susan Ferguson.
A wise and gentle woman who serves the Lord by
treating the wounded and equipping them
with the tools to get back into the battle.

Thank you to the authors of these prayers and thoughts:

Dr. Neil T. Anderson
Taken from: DAILY IN CHRIST
Copyright © 1993 by Harvest House Publishers,
Eugene, Oregon 97402
www.harvesthousepublishers.com
Used by Permission. Not to be reproduced.

"In Christ" Taken from: VICTORY OVER THE DARKNESS, p. 38-39
Copyright © 2013 by Gospel Light/Regal Books,
Ventura, CA 93003.
Used by Permission.

Brother Andrew
Open Doors Ministry, www.opendoorsusa.org
Used by Permission.

Dr. Mark I. Bubeck
Used by Permission.

Nancy Leigh DeMoss
Revive Our Hearts Ministry. www.reviveourhearts.com
Used by Permission.

Dr. C. Fred Dickason
Biblical Ministries
Used by Permission.

Rev. Paul Estabrooks
Open Doors Ministry. www.opendoorsusa.org
Used by Permission.

Dr. Erwin W. Lutzer
Moody Church, Chicago, www.moodychurch.org
Used by Permission.

Stormie Omartian
Taken from: PRAYER WARRIOR
Copyright © 2013 by Stormie Omartian
Published by Harvest House Publishers, Eugene, Oregon 97402
www.harvesthousepublishers.com
Used by Permission.

Dr. Ray Pritchard
Keep Believing Ministries, Dallas TX, www.keepbelieving.com
Used by Permission.

Dr. Marcus Warner
A Deeper Walk International, www.deeperwalkinternational.com
Used by Permission.

Thank you to these great men and women, past and present,
for their quotations and thoughts:

*Stephen Carpenter; Oswald Chambers; Jim Cymbala; John Eldredge; William Gurnall;
Madame Guyon; Dr. J. H. Jowett; C.S. Lewis; Life of Praise; Jim Logan; Max Lucado;
Martin Luther; Mary, Queen of Scots; Victor M. Matthews; J. R. Miller; Beth Moore;
George Müller; Karl Payne; Eugene H. Peterson; A.B. Simpson; Laura A. Barter Snow;
Charles H. Spurgeon; Charles R. Swindoll; J.R.R. Tolkien; R.A. Torrey; A.W. Tozer;
Timothy M. Warner; C. G. Trumbull; Philip Yancey; and Edward Young.
Every effort has been made to track down the unknown authors.*

ISBN: 978-0-578-14260-9

©2014 by Kathryn McBride
All Rights Reserved.

Published by

Letcetera
PUBLISHING
CHICAGO

www.letcecterapublishing.com

"There is only Christ, He is everything."
Colossians 3:11

CONTENTS

HOW TO USE THESE PRAYERS

Kathryn has collected these prayers and arranged them for times of definite spiritual warfare. These petitions were written by men and women who know Scripture well and are thoroughly grounded in the Word of God.

This is warfare prayer, and warfare prayer requires focus, clarity and precise thinking. There is an urgency here, because warfare is desperate. When we speak to God in the midst of our battles, we must remember that we are speaking to the very God Who commands all spiritual forces in the heavenly realms.

As a young woman, I was initially fearful of using written prayers, concerned that doing so could deaden me from hearing the Holy Spirit. I was so mistaken. I discovered instead that they expressed the words I truly wanted to say. These pattern prayers were instructive to me, not restrictive as I had feared, and gave me a concise way to communicate the words of my heart into concrete petitions. How comforting to have them to rely upon in crisis, bolstering my faith when I realized that it pleased God to come before Him in a doctrinally sound and heartfelt way. My soul was in agreement with what was already written, and I felt connected to other saints who had gone through many similar experiences. I found it especially helpful to use these prayers with an open Bible, as the Lord often brought verses to my mind.

This book is divided into sections. The first section, written by Dr. Marcus Warner, is entitled "What Every Christian Should Know About Spiritual Warfare." Next, we find Chapter One, *The Armor of God*. Here you will find a collection of prayers specifically designed to help "put on the full armor." I would suggest beginning there, choosing one of the many prayers provided and pray through one each day. In the

1

following sections, you will find chapters organized around life's daily battles, with specific prayers for yourself and others.

A Warrior's Prayerbook should be considered a resource for prayers. If you would like to know more about spiritual warfare, please read any of the wonderful books authored by the men and women found within these pages.

We hope you will take these prayers and use them to "fight on your knees," just as these prayers were intended to be prayed. How wonderful it will be to have a supplication right at your fingertips that expresses your heart's cry to God! Our earnest desire is that this collection will aid and comfort you as you intercede on behalf of others, and that it will be a personal help as you face the various trials and temptations that are common to us all.

—*Susan Ferguson*

INTRODUCTION

"Now war arose in heaven, Michael and his angels fighting against the dragon. And the dragon and his angels fought back, but he was defeated, and there was no longer any place for them in heaven. And the great dragon was thrown down, that ancient serpent, who is called the devil and Satan, the deceiver of the whole world—he was thrown down to the earth, and his angels were thrown down with him. And I heard a loud voice in heaven, saying, "Now the salvation and the power and the kingdom of our God and the authority of his Christ have come, for the accuser of our brothers has been thrown down, who accuses them day and night before our God. And they have conquered him by the blood of the Lamb and by the word of their testimony, for they loved not their lives even unto death. Therefore, rejoice, O heavens and you who dwell in them! But woe to you, O earth and sea, for the devil has come down to you in great wrath, because he knows that his time is short!" And when the dragon saw that he had been thrown down to the earth, he pursued the woman who had given birth to the male child. But the woman was given the two wings of the great eagle so that she might fly from the serpent into the wilderness, to the place where she is to be nourished for a time, and times, and half a time. The serpent poured water like a river out of his mouth after the woman, to sweep her away with a flood. But the earth came to the help of the woman, and the earth opened its mouth and swallowed the river that the dragon had poured from his mouth. *Then the dragon became furious with the woman and went off to make war on the rest of her offspring, on those who keep the commandments of God and hold to the testimony of Jesus."*
— Revelation 12:7-17 (ESV)

Satan hates us and wants to destroy us — because God loves us. We have been given the unique gift of bearing His image *(Genesis 1:26-27)*. We know that those who belong to Him have been known and loved by Him since before the foundation of the world *(Ephesians 1:4)*. He knit us together in our mother's womb *(Psalm 139:13)* and engraved our names in the palms of His hands *(Isaiah 49:16)*. Even though we lived in a state of great rebellion against Him, God demonstrated this love by sending His only Son to redeem us by bearing our curse on the cross of Calvary *(Romans 5:8)*. Simply stated, He paid our debt for us knowing we were unable to. Once His redeeming work was completed on the tree, Jesus arose from the grave and with a great thunderclap of power proclaimed His victory over death and Hell, once and for all *(2 Timothy 1:10)*. This risen Lord now is seated at the right hand of God the Father and even now is interceding on behalf of His holy ones *(Romans 8:34)*. We who have been redeemed have also been adopted as sons and daughters and have been given His Holy Spirit as a seal until He calls us home *(Ephesians 1:5; 13-14)*. This crucified and risen Lord is the Alpha and the Omega, the beginning and the end *(Revelation 1:8)*. He is the great I AM *(John 8:58)*. In Him is found the expression of the full radiance of the glory of God *(Hebrews 1:3)* as the heavenly hosts continually cry unto Him, Holy, Holy, Holy *(Revelation 4:8)*.

Is it any surprise that Satan wants to destroy us? When we took our first breath, we were born into this war — a war that has been raging since that first attempted *coup d'état*. We often cannot see the battle because it is not of flesh and blood. However, we do see the effects of this war: nations rage against nations, Christians are persecuted throughout the world, violence in the streets, deceit, selfishness, addictions, pride, rebellion, fear, disease, exploitation, isolation, death and destroyed innocence. Get the picture? So, what is it that we should do? We should pray. We need to gather our weapons and get in the trenches. In this war, if you are not a warrior, you *will* become a casualty.

All warriors receive orders. God has given us our orders through the Scriptures. Jesus said, "Behold, I am sending you out as sheep in the midst of wolves, so be wise as serpents and innocent as doves" *(Matthew 10:16)*. In this battle, warriors must be wise and brave. Warriors do not stand in the battle defenseless, because God Himself has provided us with all we need to fight. He has given us weapons, such as the "belt of truth" so that we can know the truth and not be a victim of Satan's lies; the "breastplate of righteousness" which is not only a gift which our Lord has given us but also a way of life to which we are called; the "sandals of peace" that we may be ever ready to advance the glorious gospel of God's grace; "the helmet of salvation" which gives the ability to look confidently into the eyes of our fierce enemy as we know that Christ has already won the war and that we have already been granted eternal life. He has also given us the "shield of faith" to protect us from Satan's fiery darts, and the "sword of the spirit" which is the Word of God *(Ephesians 6)*. Remember, nothing can touch us unless God permits. God is totally aware of what we are enduring at any given moment. He is not a passive Being that stands and watches what happens from the sidelines *(Isaiah 43:1-3)*. He is actively involved in the believer's life and has promised that He will never leave or forsake us *(Hebrews 13:5)*. He is here with us and understands our suffering as He was tempted in every way as we are. As a result, we never face a trial or tribulation in which He is not present with us. He knows how deep the hurts go and how hard the blows feel.... He knows *(Hebrews 4:15)*.

Can we hide from this battle? Many people try to ignore Satan — hoping that if they do he will go away and leave them alone. But does he go away? My friend, Satan is alive and well and prowling among us *(1 Peter 5:8)*. But we are not powerless! If you are a believer, you are seated positionally with Christ at the right hand of the Father right now *(Colossians 3:1, Ephesians 2:6)*. I would encourage you to take your stand, engage in the battle and trust in His power.

If you are not a believer, I have good news for you — there is a God Who loves you. He is holy and there is no one else like Him. In our rebellion, we sinned against Him and have been severed from His fellowship *(Genesis 3, Romans 3:23)*. The punishment for our sin is eternal death and separation from His presence *(Genesis 3 and Romans 6:23)*. But God in His great love for us sent His Son to the world to rescue us from our sins, while we were His enemies, by paying our penalty so that our sins would be forgiven *(Romans 5:8-10, 4:25, 2 Corinthians 5:21)*. I would urge you to repent of your sins

(Acts 3:19) and call upon the name of Jesus and trust Him as your Savior *(Romans 10:13)*. Even now you can walk with the God of the universe and know for certain that you will spend all of eternity with Him.

I've divided this book into four sections:

1. An *Introduction to Spiritual Warfare* written by Dr. Marcus Warner. Sort of a "Spiritual Warfare 101" for anyone desiring a quick primer on the subject.

2. Prayers written by true warriors of God. I thank them for allowing me to include them in this book.

3. Scriptures that have helped me through some very difficult days.

4. Thoughts from great men and women, past and present, which have particularly impacted me in those times where I have found myself in life's trenches.

This book began as a personal project as I collected prayers and Scripture that helped me in my personal journey. As time went on, my friends began asking for copies … and soon my little book began to take on a life of its own. Since then, I have watched it grow into a spiritual resource prayer book that has helped many others. In the table of contents you will find a listing of every prayer. It is important to mention that there is nothing magical about these prayers. It is Christ alone who can strike a blow against the enemy. Erwin Lutzer once said, "Only desperate people learn to pray" and I've found that to be true in my life. It is my wholehearted desire to never again face a day without putting on my spiritual armor *(Ephesians 6:10-18)* and preparing for battle.

A colonel in the United States Marines once said to me: "Make a plan… gather your troops … and draw your saber."

Sounds like good advice. Who's with me?

—Kathryn McBride

EPHESIANS 6:10-18

A final word: Be strong in the Lord and in his mighty power. Put on all of God's armor so that you will be able to stand firm against all strategies of the devil. For we are not fighting against flesh-and-blood enemies, but against evil rulers and authorities of the unseen world, against mighty powers in this dark world, and against evil spirits in the heavenly places.

Therefore, put on every piece of God's armor so you will be able to resist the enemy in the time of evil. Then after the battle you will still be standing firm. Stand your ground, putting on the belt of truth and the body armor of God's righteousness. For shoes, put on the peace that comes from the Good News so that you will be fully prepared. In addition to all of these, hold up the shield of faith to stop the fiery arrows of the devil. Put on salvation as your helmet, and take the sword of the Spirit, which is the word of God.

Pray in the Spirit at all times and on every occasion. Stay alert and be persistent in your prayers for all believers everywhere.

THE BELT OF TRUTH

THE BREASTPLATE OF RIGHTEOUSNESS

THE SHOES OF PEACE

THE SHIELD OF FAITH

THE HELMET OF SALVATION

THE SWORD OF THE SPIRIT

INTRODUCTION TO

SPIRITUAL WARFARE

Dr. Marcus Warner

Spiritual Warfare is not an optional activity for believers. It is not a program in the church you can sign up for or choose to ignore. You have not been granted immunity or vaccinated against the effects of the devil by an injection of the Holy Spirit. We live in a world at war. We have no choice in the matter. We were born into the middle of a great cosmic conflict that affects every area of life. As Christians, we really have only two options. We can live in fear and ignorance or learn to fight. So, where in the Bible does it say, "Ignore the devil and he will leave you alone?" Nowhere! It warns us repeatedly, "Be alert! Be prepared! Put on your armor! Resist!" These are not passive words. We are called to be intentional and diligent in preparing ourselves for battle. It is time for the church to wake up to the reality of the war and prepare its people and its leaders for battle.

My experience with spiritual warfare began at the age of seven. I saw a demon in my dining room staring at me. It was a big, black thing with red eyes. As you can imagine it freaked me out, and I started to scream. The others who were with me couldn't see it, but the thing was not just a vague image; it seemed to be physically present in the room. Since then I have met other children who have had night time visitors and lived with paranormal activity in their homes. A friend once called me because his son was afraid to sleep in his room. It seemed he was seeing an old woman in a rocking chair show up from time to time. He wanted to know if I thought it was just the boy's imagination or if it could be a demonic manifestation. I told him that it could definitely be demonic and counseled him to cleanse the boy's room by renouncing any claim the enemy had to the house, commanding that any spirits assigned to the place or to his son leave, and inviting Jesus to fill the house and especially that room with his presence. Several years have since passed and they have never had another issue with strange visitors in their house.

The demon that I saw in my house showed up the week after my parents' encounter with this wicked spirit. It was an act of intimidation. My dad put it this way. Satan was offering him a deal: "You leave me alone and I'll leave you alone. And you better leave me alone because if you don't, look what I can do to your kids!" The devil was trying to get at my parents through me. Thankfully, my parents were wise and courageous enough to realize that you do not make deals with the devil. You resist him. My parents began to teach me how to fight by using Scripture and praying in the name of Jesus. The demon came back one night, but I was prepared and he was quickly evicted. Who knew that resisting the devil would work better than screaming and hiding?

Pastors and Spiritual Warfare

Sadly, too few Christians are trained for war. It is even hard to find pastors who know what to do with the enemy. Our seminaries and Bible colleges rarely deal with this subject in a practical way, and many actually teach dangerously untrue paradigms about spiritual warfare that warn people away from involvement with the subject.

I received a phone call from a young pastor who was facing a crisis. It turned out there was a person in his office rolling around on the floor with demonic noises emanating through her. This pastor had been trained at a nationally recognized seminary, but one that promotes the NANC[1] form of biblical counseling to the exclusion of all others.

---

[1]NANC stands for National Association of Nouthetic Counselors. They practice a form of biblical counseling that has much to commend it. However, historically they have fought against the idea that Christians can be demonized.

Nothing in seminary or ministry training had prepared him for this. He told me that he had commanded the demon to leave in the name of Jesus, but with no effect. He had tried reading Scripture out loud but it was only making the situation worse. I gave him a crash course on spiritual warfare right there on the phone! "Authority alone won't work," I told him. "You will just wear yourself out and leave discouraged and defeated. Use your authority to bind the demons in the name of Jesus. Command them to be silent and inactive and to allow you to speak to the woman who came to you for help."

I listened as the pastor did this and could hear him gaining control of the situation. He was soon able to speak with the woman and would periodically repeat his command to silence the wicked spirit. I then told him that this kind of demonic episode usually only happens if there has been significant occult involvement by the person themselves or their family. I encouraged him to ask if she had ever dabbled in the occult and if so, to renounce each area of participation and to use her authority as a Christian to command the demons who had gained access through her participation to leave. He already knew that she had been raised in a family where the occult was commonly practiced and that she herself had often participated in tarot card readings, Ouija boards and other forms of witchcraft.

To his credit, the pastor handled the situation beautifully. Once he got the basic concepts in mind of using authority to bind, renouncing the sins that had opened the door to the demons , and assisting the woman to use her own authority in Christ to evict them, they started making headway. He called me back a few days later and said that over the course of two sessions they believed the woman was completely free of the demons. They were now working on discipling her in order to build her up in the faith. However, he had two very good questions, "Why was I taught that stuff like this can't happen to Christians? And, where do I go to learn how to help people in this condition?" I was able to direct him to Mark Bubeck's book, *The Adversary* and to one co-authored by my father and Neil Anderson, *The Beginner's Guide to Spiritual Warfare*. A few months later he and his wife came to one of our training courses and told me about the many victories they were beginning to see and how much he was growing as he continued on this journey.

In this section I want to explain the two most basic principles of spiritual warfare ministry: legal ground and authority. If you get a handle on these two concepts and how they relate to one another, it will go a long way to helping you understand the spiritual battle in which we find ourselves.

LEGAL GROUND

Legal ground is permission to act. Demons need permission to do whatever they do. At the beginning of this age, God decreed that Satan and his demons are free to roam the earth. However, they are not free to do whatever they want to do, or we would all be dead. Satan had to get permission to attack Job *(Job 1-2)*. He had to ask to "sift" Peter *(Luke 22:31)*. In the same way, demons need legal permission from the court of heaven to oppress people or rule territory. In the last days God will give Satan permission to make war with his saints and overcome them *(Revelation 13:7)*. Satan will be given a legal right to do this for a limited amount of time and in a limited way, simply because of God's decree. But there are also times when we give the devil permission to act in our lives because of the choices we make. When we sin or when we enter into agreements with the devil, we give him a legal right to greater activity in our lives than he would otherwise have.

Whole populations who live in a particular region (such as countries, provinces, or districts) can give permission for greater activity to demons when their leaders enter into covenants with false gods. When Moab chose to make Chemosh its god *(Number 21:29)*, it gave the demons associated with that god permission to a far greater degree of activity in their country than they would have had without the idolatry of the people. In the same way, individuals, even Christians, can make choices that give demons a legal right to be active in their lives.

The point is this. If a demon has a legal right to be somewhere, you can't just come along and say, "In the name of Jesus you have to leave." It would be like trying to evict someone from a house who has a contract giving them a legal right to be there. If you want to get rid of them, you have to remove the "legal ground" they claim. People who find themselves in long, shouting matches with demons that drag on for hours have trouble because they are trying to evict a demon that has a legal right to be where it is. No amount of shouting "In the name of Jesus I command you to leave" is going to make it leave. Most of what happens in a biblically-balanced, practical approach to deliverance takes place at the level of removing legal ground. Once that is done, the evicting is generally pretty easy. Removing legal ground is essentially a matter of confessing sins, forgiving debts or renouncing lies and then canceling the demonic claims that were based on those sins, debts, and lies.

Christians and Demons. I once gave a talk on spiritual warfare to a group of high school students titled, "How to make the devil your roommate." In the talk I introduced them to four doors we often open that invite the devil into our lives, often without even realizing what we have done. The four doors can be remembered with the word *SOUL*. They are sin (S), occult (O), unforgiveness (U), and lineage (L). The biblical principle here is often called legal ground. It is rooted in Paul's statement in Ephesians 4:27 that believers can give the devil a place in their lives. The word translated "place" refers to ground or territory that we surrender to the devil by the choices we make. It is called legal ground because the devil needs to gain legal permission to be there from the court of heaven. The Bible clearly teaches that God is sovereign. He sits on his throne and the whole world is subject to him, including the devil. For His own purposes and glory, God has decreed that in this present, evil age Satan is to have a limited amount of freedom to roam this earth and challenge God's glory here. Just as Satan sought permission to sift Peter *(Matthew 26)* and attack Job *(Job 1,2)*, he needs legal permission to do whatever he does. We often inadvertently give him the legal right to be more active in our lives than he otherwise would be by our participation in sin, the occult, unforgivness, and embracing his lies as the truth. When we do these things, we give him legal ground that opens the door for his activity in our lives. This is why legal ground is sometimes referred to as surrendered ground.

The question is often asked, "How can a Christian have a demon?" It is really not that difficult of a question to answer, if you get the right paradigm in place. Our problem is that we have tended to adopt a possession or oppression model for understanding the issue that warps the discussion. For one thing, the word possession never occurs in the Bible. It began when the translators of the King James Version came to the Greek word *daimonizomai* and instead of creating a new English word "demonized" directly from the Greek as they did with the noun form of the same word, they used the word "possessed" in an attempt to translate it. There is nothing in the word *daimonizomai* that implies possession. Possession refers to ownership, and Christians are "owned" by the Lord Jesus Christ who bought us with his blood. Christians cannot be "possessed" in this sense of the word. However, Christians can be demonized. This is why Paul warns the Corinthians that participating in the occult worship practices of the pagans will cause them to have "fellowship" *(koinonia)* with demons *(1 Corinthians 10:20-22)*. When a Christian starts to have "fellowship" with demons, he is opening the door to all sorts of problems. Let me share a word picture of how this works.

The Temple — In Ezekiel 8-10 the Spirit of the Lord gave the prophet a vision of the abominations that were taking place in His temple. He saw the seventy elders of Israel offering incense to pagan gods. He saw the women of Israel performing the ritual mourning for Tammuz (a

Babylonian god whose mythological story has him dying in battle only to be raised to life by his consort Ishtar; similar to the mythological stories of Baal and Asherah in Canaan and Osiris and Isis in Egypt). It was believed that performing the mourning rituals would bring blessing and fertility to the land and families of the worshipers. In the inner court, Ezekiel saw 25 men bowing down to the sun in worship. Outside the temple, the city itself was filled with violence and perversion. Yet while all of this was going on the Shekinah glory was still in the Holy of Holies. In chapter ten the prophet describes in great detail the departure of God's presence and throne from the temple, so that it could be destroyed. Can you see how God's presence and the unholy presence of demonic entities could be in the same temple at the same time? God was present in the innermost court, while in the outer courts demons were being summoned by the rituals being performed. It is the same with a Christian. God's Spirit may live in our hearts, but that does not mean that in our flesh we cannot give a place for demons to reside.

How do we get out of this? I deal with that question more fully in my booklet, *What Every Believer Should Know About Spiritual Warfare*. For now, my hope is that these analogies have helped you see how Christians can surrender "ground" in a way that gives the devil a legal right to a place to their lives. In *Waking the Dead* John Eldredge puts it this way:

> *What (Satan) is seeking is a sort of 'agreement' on our part. He's hoping we'll buy into whatever he's saying, offering, insinuating. Our first parents bought into it, and look what disaster came of it. But that story is not over. The Evil One is still lying to us, seeking our agreement every single day (152).*

He goes on to write,

> *The whole plan is based on agreements. When we make those agreements with the demonic forces suggesting things to us, we come under their influence. It becomes a kind of permission we*

give the enemy, sort of like a contract. The bronze gates start clanging shut around us. I'm serious—maybe half the stuff people are trying to 'work through' in counseling offices, or pray about in their quiet times, is simply agreements they've made with the Enemy (154-155).

Can you see how a basic understanding of the devil's schemes in this area can help us recognize what is going on in our lives so that we can begin to fight it with the proper weapons and strategies?

AUTHORITY

When I was a child my parents taught me to stand against harassment from wicked spirits by saying, "In the name of Jesus I command you to leave." At the time, I felt like a sheriff out in the Wild West telling the bad guys, "Stop, in the name of the Law." My parents explained to me that I was not standing against the demons in my own name or in my own power. I was standing against them in the name and power of Jesus in the same way that David stood against Goliath in the name and power of the Lord. If it was David against Goliath, Goliath would win every time. But it was Goliath against the Most High God. David was simply the representative that God chose to use.

To act in the name of Jesus is to act within the boundaries of the authority he has delegated to us. To do something "in His name" is to do it as His representative in the same way that a sheriff represents the local government. As a child, it was obvious to me that the demons had more power than I did. If the contest was between my power and their power, they would win every time. But when I came against the enemy in the name of Jesus, they had to listen because, if they chose to mess with me, they knew they were picking a fight with Jesus. It would be like me being pulled over by a police officer and saying, "Oh, it's just Joe. He's not a very good police officer and he's an even worse father and husband. I don't have to listen to him." His authority in that setting has nothing to do with his competence or his character. It has to do with the government he represents. If he is within the bounds of the law in his dealings with me, he has authority over me. In the same way, Christians are like police officers. Whether we are one day out of the academy or a thirty year veteran, we all have the same authority. Some are just more experienced at using it.

The Christian's authority over demons is not a spiritual gift. Don't fall into the trap of thinking that some Christians have this authority and some do not. The authority of the believer is rooted in the fact that we are in Christ, and in Christ we are seated with Him in the heavenly realms far above the angels, whether evil or elect. When Jesus defeated Satan at the cross and rose again, He was given a name above every name *(Philippians 2:9)*. This is why Jesus told His disciples, "All authority in heaven and on earth has been given unto me" *(Matthew 28:18-19)*. Our Lord has been given the highest position of authority in the universe. In Christ, a measure of that authority has been delegated to us to wield in harmony with His will and purposes.

The following diagram illustrates our position of authority. Humans were made "a little lower than the angels." The stars represent the angels and the upside down dark star represents Satan and his demons.

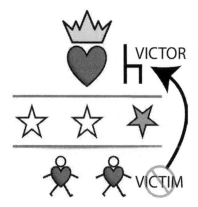

If I were to take on the Adversary in my own strength, he would be in a position of dominance over me. Unfortunately, many Christians live this way. It keeps us in the position of "victim." If we believe this to be true, it will rob us of one of our greatest resources and leave us defeated and discouraged. However, Jesus made himself a little lower than the angels and became a human. Not only that, He made Himself our servant. What is more, He laid down His life for us and died for the sins of the whole world. In this way He disarmed the angelic hosts that were at war against Him. He defeated Satan and robbed him of the keys to death and Hades. He then rose to life and ascended to heaven where God seated Him far above all principalities and powers. In Ephesians 2:6 we read that God raised us up together with Christ and seated us together with Him in heavenly places. From this position at the right hand of the father we have intimacy with God and authority over the enemy. We no longer struggle as victims, but we wage war as victors.

There are two equal and opposite errors into which Christians sometimes fall with regard to authority. First, there are those who believe that Christians have NO authority. These people often point to a text like Jude in which Michael did not rebuke Lucifer, but said, "The Lord rebuke you." They argue that if Michael, who is greater than we are, did not have authority over Lucifer, how could we? Now that you have seen the authority diagram of our position in Christ, how would you answer that question? Hopefully, you would recognize that Michael and Lucifer are equals in authority. The angels, even archangels, are not seated with Christ at the right hand of God the Father Almighty. It should also be pointed out that the humans discussed in Jude's letter are false teachers, who are not Christians at all, and therefore have no claim to authority. This passage should be understood in the context of an apostle who is "contending for the faith" against mockers who have infiltrated the flock like wolves in sheep's clothing. Jude's primary purpose is not to address the issue of authority but to point out the arrogance of these false teachers.

Second, there are those who believe that Christians have ALL authority. Our authority as Christians is limited by law. We do not have unlimited authority. If we did, we could just go into any hospital and say, "In the name of Jesus everybody is healed." Or we could go to a Hindu temple and cast out all of the demonic spirits. If we spoke, it would be as if Jesus were speaking. But we can only use our authority to the limit that the decrees and laws of the courtroom of heaven allow us to use it. For example, if a police officer pulls you over and says, "I'm sorry. You were going fifteen miles an hour over the speed limit, I have to give you a ticket," she has every right to that. But if the same officer pulls you over and says, "I'm sorry, but your breath stinks, I am giving you a ticket," well, she doesn't have the authority to do that. Her authority is limited by the law. If the law says there is a speed limit and you violate the limit, a police officer can give you a ticket; and if you resist her authority, you will find yourself fighting, not just the officer, but all the power of the government represented by the officer. In the same way, I can use my authority over a demon if that demon is doing something it has no right to do. But if the demon has "legal ground," I can't evict it simply because I feel like it. Before I can tell it to leave, I have to reclaim the surrendered ground.

Uses of Authority

There are three primary uses of authority as a believer: (1) binding, (2) loosing, and (3) evicting.

Binding — The Greek word "binding" is *deo* and "loosing" is *luo. Deo* is normally used for securing prisoners by tying them with ropes or putting them in irons. It was also used of binding together sheaves of grain. Jesus said that we sometimes must bind the strongman in order to rob his house. In spiritual warfare, we do this by using our authority to bind the enemy so that the person we are trying to help can function enough to express their will. Many times I have seen people who were unable to complete their prayers or verbalize their renunciations of the legal ground being claimed by the enemy, until that enemy was bound in the name of Jesus.

A young man once came to see me who was struggling in his attempts to disciple a friend. Even though he had years of experience in discipling others through the Campus Ministry he helped to lead, he wasn't having any success with his friend. "I don't get it" he said. "This man is a veterinarian. He's smart, he's successful, but whenever we talk about the Bible, he can't seem to follow the simplest line of thought. I've tried everything." Then he looked at me with a look of understanding and added, "except spiritual warfare." He then asked me what to do. I told him, "The next time you meet with this man, during your opening prayer, bind any demons from interfering with his ability to process what he is learning or any work that God wants to do." He wasn't sure how to do that; so I let him know that it was as simple as saying the words, "In the name of Jesus I bind any demons from interfering." He said he would give it a try. The next Sunday at church, he came up to me with a look of amazement on his face. "You won't believe it," he said. "Not only did my friend interact intelligently with the study this time, we found out that his family has been practicing the occult for generations and that he has secretly practiced homosexuality for over seven years." That made sense. Both of those things would give legal ground to the enemy to harass this man. "So, what do I do now?" my friend asked. I pointed him to Neil Anderson's book *The Bondage Breaker* and told him to take his friend through the *Steps to Freedom in Christ*. That day, this young man who was an expert in discipling others according to the traditional discipling models started a journey of his own that opened up areas in his own life in which he was living in bondage and needed to be free. I was able to take him through the *Steps to Freedom* as well and help him get grounded in the basics of heart-focused discipleship.

There are many times when I am helping someone work through their baggage that we get interference from the enemy. I routinely stop and bind demons from interfering before we move on. It is amazing how dramatic the change can be. Once, a woman was in the midst of forgiving someone for sexually abusing her when a black box appeared and blocked her memory of the event. We both thought that was odd, so I led her to pray, "In the name of Jesus, if this black box is from the enemy to interfere with what we are doing, I command them to remove it now and to stop interfering." Immediately, the black box disappeared and she completed a time with the Lord that led to great healing in her heart. Another time, a person was having trouble getting the words out when he was renouncing his involvement with the occult. He would start to say, "I renounce S---------," but he couldn't get the rest of it out. (I have actually seen this dozens of times). We simply paused and bound the demons that were interfering, and he was able to finish his prayer. Once you deal with this often enough, you learn to simply open your sessions with prayer by binding the enemy to inactivity and to obedience to the commands of Christ. A good and very thorough model for such a prayer can be found in Karl Payne's book *Spiritual Warfare* (see a form of this prayer on page 128).

Loosing — Binding is something Christians use their authority to do to demons, loosing is something we do for ourselves and others. To loose is to undo bonds. It is removing the cords that demons have used to keep people in bondage. We can do this through forgiveness. Forgiving removes the bonds of bitterness that keep us spiritually connected to someone who has wronged us. We can also do this by canceling "soul ties." A soul tie is a demonic bond that connects two people together. It is usually formed by the shared experience of sin. It may be that the people sinned together, perhaps by engaging in sex outside of marriage or by committing a crime together. But it may also be that one person sinned against another through abuse or some other unwanted behavior. A friend of mine was explaining soul ties to a buddy of his who had engaged in sexual relations with several women during his lifetime. Now that he was married, he was having trouble not thinking about other women when he was with his wife and struggling with lust in general. My friend told him to renounce any soul ties that had been formed with the other women and to command any demons that were keeping him bound to them to leave. The next time he saw him, he said that he had significantly more freedom than before, but that there was one woman with whom it didn't seem to work. After discussing this briefly, my friend realized that there was a different kind of soul tie with this woman. The young man he was helping had come to worship her as a goddess. She was his fantasy—his dream girl; and he not only had to renounce his sexual activity with her, he had to renounce the idolatry that had placed her on a pedestal above all others. That turned out to be the "legal ground" that needed to be reclaimed; and, as soon as he did that, he experienced a tremendous sense of freedom. He had been loosed from bondage.

Evicting — Not only is authority used for binding and loosing. Authority is used to evict wicked spirits.

This process can be explained with two simple memory devices. The first is comes from Karl Payne's book, *Spiritual Warfare: Christians, demonization, and deliverance.* It is *CCC: Confess, Cancel, and Command.* The second is my summary of what we as Christians often do that gives demons permission to a place in our lives. It is *SOUL: sin, occult, unforgiveness, and lineage.* These are the most common doorways that give legal ground to the enemy.

C.C.C. — Karl Payne uses a simple three-step process for evicting demonic spirits that is easy to remember. It is the three Cs: Confess, Cancel, and Command. First, you confess the sin; then you cancel any claim the demons may have based on that sin; and then you command the demons to leave. When demons know that they have no more legal ground, and when they know that you know they have no more legal ground, it is usually not difficult to make them leave. The problems tend to arise when you don't remove the legal ground.

S.O.U.L. — In an earlier chapter I introduced four doorways that give the devil a place in our lives: Sin, the Occult, Unforgiveness, and Lineage. Each of these issues has a remedy. The remedy for sin is repentance. The remedy for the occult is renunciation. The remedy for unforgiveness is forgiveness and the remedy for sins that come to us through our family line is to cut them off.

Neil Anderson's *Steps to Freedom* is a comprehensive inventory of the seven most common areas in which we surrender legal ground to the devil (occult, deception, bitterness, pride, rebellion, habitual sin, and generational sin). It is an excellent tool for walking yourself or someone else through the renunciations and prayers most commonly required to reclaim surrendered ground.

Sin — Ephesians 4:26 says that sin gives the devil a foothold in your life. To reclaim ground surrendered to the enemy through sin, we simply have to confess that sin. If a demon did enter a person on the basis of the legal ground given by that sin, confession cancels the demon's claim. However, that does not mean that the demon automatically leaves. Demons often have to be evicted. It is no different than sending a notice to a renter who refuses to pay their lease that they have been evicted and sending the police to enforce the notice and forcibly evict the squatters. Confession is like going to the courtroom of heaven to get the eviction notice. It cancels their legal claim to a place in your life. But sometimes you have to call in the police. You do this by actively addressing the demons and commanding them to leave in the name of Jesus. Sometimes I have even asked Jesus to send holy angels to escort them out. (I don't command holy angels to do anything. It doesn't seem appropriate. But I often ask Jesus for angelic support!)

A sample prayer for confessing and canceling legal ground:

> *"In the name of Jesus, I confess my participation in _____.*
> *I renounce my participation in this sin and hereby cancel the*
> *ground in my life claimed by my enemy. In the name of Jesus,*

I now command every demon who took advantage of this ground to renounce their claim on me and leave. You must go where the Lord Jesus sends you."

Occult — If sin opens the door to the devil, then the occult is like opening a garage door. It is sin that puts you directly into contact with the demonic.

Ending Satan's claim on your life because of occult activity begins with the three C's. You must confess that you did it, cancel any claim the Enemy may have on you, and command the demons to leave. It is sometimes also necessary to destroy the occult objects you own or that have been used to grant them access to your world. One tribal priest whose family had served a pagan god in Africa for ten generations made a decisive break with his occult background. He gave his life to Christ and got baptized, then went to the ritual site where the idol was located. He announced to the spirit that he would no longer serve him. He destroyed the idol and burned it in a fire, then for good measure he sprayed his own urine all over the "sacred" site. Now, that is what I would call a full renunciation of one's occult involvement!

Unforgiveness — The obvious antidote to unforgiveness is forgiveness. There are a few principles about forgiveness, however, that are worth mentioning. First, forgiveness is a choice not a feeling. When you forgive someone, you are canceling the debt that is owed to you. In this sense it is a business transaction. You might picture yourself in front of a judge who is asking you, "Are you going to cancel the debt or not?" Your emotions don't really enter into it from a legal perspective. However, the Bible tells us to forgive others "from the heart." This does not mean that we have to wait to choose to forgive them until we feel like forgiving them. It means that we need to get in touch with our feelings when we forgive and not simply say the words out of obligation. God does not want us to simply go through the motions, nor does he want us to simply pretend everything is okay. He wants us to trust Him to take care of us and leave the debt and the right to vengeance in His hands.

Another important principle about forgiveness is that it is not the same as reconciliation. Reconciliation takes two. Forgiveness only takes one. You can cancel a debt without the other person being in the courtroom. Reconciliation, however, is the reestablishment of a relationship and the rebuilding of trust. Without forgiveness, reconciliation will not be possible, but forgiveness alone does not produce reconciliation. This was driven home to me by the story of a pastor who was called to a home where the wife had just found out that her husband had been cheating on her with a close friend. All sorts of scenarios ran through this pastor's mind of what he would find when he arrived. What he found, however, was nothing like what he had expected. When he arrived, the husband was angry with the wife, rather than the other way around! The husband was angry because his wife would not "forgive" him. The man told the pastor, "Tell my wife she needs to forgive me. Tell her she needs to give me a kiss, put this behind us, and go on like it never happened." This husband actually believed this would be the biblical thing to do! The reality is that he was confusing forgiveness with reconciliation, and in the process was trying to absolve himself of any consequences for what he had done. Forgiveness does not mean there will be no consequences. I can forgive my child for rebellion against me. It doesn't mean there won't be a time out or worse. The discipline is part of the restoration process. There are times when mercy will reduce punishment or even remove it, but this is not required by forgiveness.

When it comes to the process of forgiving I encourage people to take the following steps:

• Ask God to help you think about the person in the way in which they are the most offensive to you. This helps you get your heart engaged, so that you can forgive from your heart.

- Reflect on the negative emotions and negative consequences you have had to bear because of what the other person has done.

- Make a declaration: "In the name of Jesus, I choose to forgive _____ for …" and list the wrong behavior and negative consequences imposed against you.

- Ask Jesus to help you think about the person in the way in which He wants you to think about them. Ask him to help you understand why He loves that person, so that you can learn to love them, too.

- Pray a blessing on the person you forgave, and ask the Lord to bring them what is good (even if that good thing is repentance that leads to life).

Lineage — In our culture, we do not often think about the impact of prior generations on our lives in the present. We are so individualistic that we forget that our lives flow out of a source (like our family tree) that often has impurities in it that affect us.

Demons from past generations can affect people in the present. Perhaps great-grandpa murdered someone, or grandma practiced witchcraft, or dad developed a porn addiction and committed adultery. Any of these sins would open a door into that person's life. As a consequence those demons will have greater access to the family lineage than if the door had not been opened. If you think of your family as being like a house, imagine what would happen if someone invited a demon into one of the rooms. Is it likely to just stay there or is it going to look for a way to stay in this home and expand its territory? In the same way, once a demon or demons have gained ground in a family, they are going to look for ways to stay and they are going to seek to expand their "territory" and freedom to operate.

One young man who needed freedom from panic attacks prayed that God would show him the first time fear had entered his life. He remembered being alone in a bathroom when he was about seven years old and feeling like something jumped on his back. He was terrified and had his first panic attack. When I asked him if any other family members struggled with fear or high levels of worry, he mentioned that both his mother and grandmother were consumed with worry. We decided it was best to renounce any ancestral sin that may have opened a door to the demonic in his family line. As I led him through the prayer, he got stuck. He began to get interference from a demon. We bound the wicked spirit, finished the prayer and evicted the spirit involved. Afterward, the young man said, "I never would have dreamed that my problems had roots in my family line."

A couple who adopted a child from a Muslim background had no end of behavioral problems with him. He was a "holy terror" and was regularly in trouble at school. They were at their wits end, when someone suggested to them that they cut off any wicked spirits that may have come with him from his ancestral background. One night, while the boy was sleeping, his parents prayed over him and canceled any claim the enemy had on their adopted son because of the sins of his ancestors, and commanded those spirits to leave in the name of Jesus. The next morning, they could already notice a difference in the level of calmness in the child. By the end of the week his teacher sent home a note saying, "I don't know what you've been doing with your son, but whatever it is, keep it up!" Dealing with the spirits that had come down through the family line did not make the boy perfect, but they did make him "normal."

Dealing with generational sin follows the same three C pattern as before. Confess the sin that gave the ground. In this case it is the sin of an ancestor. You can confess all sins generally that have given ground whether you know about the sin or not, but it is a good idea to list the ones of which you are specifically aware especially if they were habitual or traumatic. Cancel the ground claimed by the enemy because of that sin. Specifically cancel any claim they may have on future generations. Command the demons to leave.

CONCLUSION

A functional knowledge of spiritual warfare is one of the foundational pillars of a Christian worldview. It is as primary to our understanding of the Christian life as the sovereignty of God or our union with Christ. In fact, I would argue that these are the three core pillars on which all Christianity rests. The first is our union with Christ, which deals with our death, resurrection, and ascension with Christ so that we now live our lives in Him and He in us. The second is the sovereignty of God, which teaches us that God is strong enough, wise enough, and good enough to use even the evil that exists and that is done in this world to advance His eternal purposes for His people. Finally, there is spiritual warfare. This doctrine teaches us that when we were adopted spiritually into God's family, we became targets of God's arch-enemy. This enemy is actively working to make sure that we do not live our lives on the foundation of the first two pillars.

This is where the Christian finds balance in the study of spiritual warfare. We need to know our enemy, understand his tactics, and be prepared to stand against him with the weapons of our warfare. But we do not live our lives focused on the enemy. We live our lives in union with Christ and by faith in the sovereignty of God. This is where our focus lies and this is the path to a deeper walk. My prayer for you is that you will not be deceived by our adversary the devil, but will learn to enjoy the simplicity, freedom, and beauty of a deeper walk with Christ.

Kathryn McBride has done a great job in this book of collecting materials from various spiritual warfare authors and making them accessible to people who find themselves in a battle and needing guidance on how to pray. If you want to dive further into your study of this subject, I would recommend the following as a great place to start.

- My short, introductory book, *What Every Believer Should Know About Spiritual Warfare*

- Timothy Warner (my father), *Spiritual Warfare* and *The Beginner's Guide to Spiritual Warfare* (with Neil T. Anderson)

- Neil T. Anderson, *Victory over the Darkness* and the *Bondage Breaker*

- Mark Bubeck, *The Adversary* and *Overcoming the Adversary*

- Karl Payne, *Spiritual Warfare: Christians, Demonization, and Deliverance*

About Marcus Warner

Dr. Marcus Warner is the president of Deeper Walk International. A graduate of Trinity Evangelical Divinity School (M.Div., Th. M., D. Min.), Dr. Warner taught Old Testament and Theology at Bethel College in Mishawaka, Indiana and later served for seven years as the senior pastor of an evangelical church in Carmel, Indiana. He has over twenty years of experience in spiritual warfare ministry. He lives in the Indianapolis area with his wife, Brenda, and two children—Stephanie and Benjamin.

Chapter One

THE ARMOR OF GOD

"Things are not what they seem…You were born into a world at war. When Satan lost the battle with Michael and his angels, 'He was hurled to the earth, and his angels with him' (Revelation 12:9). That means that right now, on this earth, there are hundreds of thousands, if not millions, of fallen angels, foul spirits, bent on our destruction. And what is Satan's mood? 'He is filled with fury, because he knows that his time is short.' (v. 12) …You have an Enemy. He is trying to steal your freedom, kill your heart, and destroy your life."

— *John Eldredge,* Waking the Dead

Standing in the Power and Armor of God

Father God, You have warned us that we do not wrestle against humans, but against spiritual forces under Satan. I would come to You for your power and strength in the battle. Enable me to stand in the power that You supply in Christ. I will not trust in my power, not even in my prayers. My strength is from You, Lord. My home is in You, Lord. See me through to victory.

I would, as you command, put on the full armor that You supply. These pieces I would put on in full confidence that they are sufficient for the battle. I know that even if there are difficult times, stresses, setbacks and even some defeats, You are the Victor, Lord Jesus, and I am the fray. I will stand clothed with the armor You supply for the heat of the battle.

Therefore, setting aside all sin, pride, self-sufficiency, and error. I would put on the whole armor of God. I recognize that through my position in the grace of Christ I already have on the first three pieces of armor. I thank you for *the belt of truth* — that I stand in the truth system that centers in the person and work of Christ. I thank you that I have *the breastplate of righteousness* — that the righteousness of Christ has been placed on my account through justification by faith. I thank you that I have *the sandals of peace* — that I stand in peace with God through faith in Christ. Even in the midst of the battle, I know God is for me and will help me because of my eternal relationship to Him through the blood of Christ.

I now take up the other three pieces of armor that you have provided. I raise *the shield of faith* — that great defense of confidence in your person and Word. With it I will ward off all the doubts and threats that the enemy would fire at me. I put on *the helmet of salvation* — that protection of hope of deliverance in the battle. I am on the winning side. God will triumph. Satan will be defeated. I can trust the Living

Lord in all my circumstances. I now pick up the *sword of the Spirit* — the sayings of the Word of God that are appropriate to my need in the battle. Your Word is true and I depend on it. I will hide it in my heart and use it boldly against all error to cut through all falsehood and opposition.

With the power of Christ and the armor of God, I stand complete. I determine, by your power and grace, to stand firm in all areas and events of life. I will trust You and You alone to care for my well-being, safety, freedom and development.

Again, I affirm my trust in the Lord Jesus as the Risen Savior, Lord and Victor over all evil. I confess and renounce all that dishonors Christ and hinders my relationship to You and my service for You. I submit to you. I resist the devil. I trust You to make Him flee from me. Grant me deliverance from any influences and any control that Satan and his demons might seek to exercise over me. My mind, my emotion, my will, my body—my whole being—is yours, Lord Jesus. Break the bondage of sin and evil and set me free to live for your honor and glory. I praise You for your goodness, grace, love, and power and believe that You will continue to deliver me and cultivate my life in your good and sovereign plan. *Amen.*

— *Dr. C. Fred Dickason*

THE ARMOR OF GOD

Lord, help me to put on the full spiritual armor You have provided for me so that I can "stand against the wiles of the devil" every day.

The Belt of Truth: Lord, show me how to gird up the core of my being with Your truth so that I don't fall into deception of any kind. Teach me to not only know Your truth, but to live in it.

The Breastplate of Righteousness: Lord, help me to put on the breastplate of righteousness that protects me from the enemy's attacks. I know it is your righteousness in me that protects me, but I also know I must not neglect to put on Your righteousness like a bulletproof vest by doing what is right in Your eyes. Reveal to me thoughts, attitudes and habits of my heart that are not pleasing to You. Show me what I have done, or am about to do, that does not glorify You. I want to see anything in me that violates Your high standards for my life so I can confess it, turn away from it, and be cleansed from all unrighteousness.

The Shoes of Peace: Thank You, Jesus, that I have peace beyond comprehension because of what You accomplished on the cross for me. Help me to stand secure with my feet protected by the good news that You have already prepared and secured for me. Because I have peace with You and from You, I am able to not only stand strong but to walk forward against the enemy and take back territory he has stolen from us all.

The Helmet of Salvation: Lord, help me to put on the helmet of salvation to protect my head and mind each day by remembering all You have saved me from, including the lies of the enemy. Enable me to remember only what You say about me and not what the enemy wants me to believe. Thank You that Your helmet of salvation protects me from warfare in my mind. Your salvation gives me everything I need in order to live successfully.

The Shield of Faith: Lord, thank You that You have given me faith and have grown my faith in Your Word. I don't have faith in my own faith, as if I have accomplished anything myself, but I have faith in You and Your faithfulness to me, which is a shield from the enemy's arrows. Just as You were Abraham's shield and David's shield, You are mine as well. Thank You that even if my faith is shaky one day, Your faithfulness never is. "O Lord of hosts, blessed is the man who trusts in You!" *(Psalm 84:12).* Help me to remember Your faithfulness at all times. You, Lord, are "my strength and my shield;" my heart trusts in You "and I am helped" *(Psalm 28:7).* Enable me to take up the shield of faith as constant protection from the enemy. My soul waits for You, Lord, my help and my shield *(Psalm 33:20).*

The Sword of the Spirit: Lord, help me to take up the sword of the Spirit every day, for Your Word not only protects me from the enemy, but it is my greatest weapon against him. Enable me to always pray as Your Spirit leads me, and to keep on praying as long as I should. Teach me to be the strong and unshakable prayer warrior You want me to be so that I can accomplish Your will. In Jesus' name I pray. *Amen.*

—*Stormie Omartian*

PRAYER TO WEAR THE ARMOR OF GOD

Heavenly Father, I put on the armor of God with gratitude and praise. You have provided all I need to stand in victory against Satan and his kingdom. I confidently take *the belt of truth.* Thank You that Satan cannot stand against the bold use of truth. Thank You for *the breastplate of righteousness.* I embrace that righteousness which is mine by faith in Jesus Christ. I know that Satan must retreat before the righteousness of God. You have provided the solid rock of peace. I claim the peace with God that is mine through justification. I desire the peace of God that touches my emotions and feelings through prayer and sanctification *(Philippians 4:6).* Eagerly, Lord I lift up *the shield of faith* against all the blazing missiles that Satan fires at me. I know that You are my shield. I recognize that my mind is a particular target of Satan's deceiving ways. I cover my mind with the powerful *helmet of salvation.* With joy I lift *the sword of the Spirit,* which is the Word of God, I choose to live in its truth and power. Enable me to use Your Word to defend myself from Satan, and also to wield the sword well, to push Satan back—to defeat him.

Thank You, dear Lord, for prayer. Help me to keep this armor well oiled with prayer. All these petitions I offer You through the mighty name of our Lord Jesus Christ. *Amen.*

—*Dr. Mark I. Bubeck*

A WARRIOR'S PRAYER

Heavenly Father, I bow in worship and praise before You. I cover myself with the blood of the Lord Jesus Christ as my protection. I surrender myself completely and unreservedly in every area of my life to You. I take a stand against all the workings of Satan that would hinder me in my prayer life. I address myself only to the True and Living God and refuse any involvement of Satan in my prayer. *Satan, I command you, in the Name of the Lord Jesus Christ, to leave my presence with all of your demons. I bring the blood of the Lord Jesus Christ between us.* Heavenly Father, I worship You and give You praise. I recognize that You are worthy to receive all glory and honor and praise. I renew my allegiance to You and pray that the blessed Holy Spirit would enable me in this time of prayer. I am thankful, Heavenly Father, that You have loved me from past eternity and that You sent the Lord Jesus Christ into the world to die as my substitute. I am thankful that the Lord Jesus Christ came as my representative and through Him; You have completely forgiven me; You have adopted me into Your family; You have assumed all responsibility for me; You have given me eternal life; You have given me the perfect righteousness of the Lord Jesus Christ so I am now justified. I am thankful that in Him You have made me complete, and that You have offered Yourself to me to be my daily help and strength. Heavenly Father, open my eyes that I might see how great You are and how complete Your provision is for this day. I am thankful that the victory the Lord Jesus Christ won for me on the Cross and in His resurrection has been given to me and that I am seated with the Lord Jesus Christ in the heavenlies. I take my place with Him in the heavenlies and recognize by faith that all wicked spirits and Satan himself are under my feet. I declare, therefore, that Satan and his wicked spirits are subject to me in the Name of the Lord Jesus Christ.

I am thankful for the Armor You have provided. I put on *the girdle of truth, the breastplate of righteousness,* and *the sandals of peace* and *the helmet of salvation.* I lift up *the shield of faith* against all the fiery darts of the enemy; and I take in my right hand *the sword of the Spirit,* the Word of God. I choose to use Your Word against all of the forces of evil in my life. I put on this Armor and live and pray in complete dependence upon You, blessed Holy Spirit. I am grateful, Heavenly Father, that the Lord Jesus Christ spoiled all principalities and powers and made a show of them openly and triumphed over them in Himself. I claim all that victory for my life today. I reject all the insinuations and accusations, and the temptations of Satan. I affirm that the Word of God is true and I choose to live today in the light of God's Word. I choose, Heavenly Father to live in obedience to You and in fellowship with Yourself. Open my eyes and show me the areas of my life that do not please You. Work in me to cleanse me from all ground that would give Satan a foothold against me. I do in every way stand into all that it means to be Your adopted child and I welcome the ministry of the Holy Spirit.

By faith and in dependence upon you, I put off the fleshly works of the old man and stand into all the victory of the crucifixion where the Lord Jesus Christ provided cleansing from my old nature. I put on the new man and stand into all the victory of the resurrection and the provision He has made for me to live above sin. Therefore, today I put off all forms of selfishness and put on the new nature with its love. I put off all forms of fear and put on the new nature with its courage. I put off all forms of weakness and put on the new nature with its strength. I put off all forms of lust and put on the new nature with its righteousness, purity, and honesty. I am trusting You to show me how to make this practical in my daily life.

In every way I stand into the Victory of the ascension and glorification of the Lord Jesus Christ, whereby all the principalities and powers were made subject to Him. I claim my place in Christ as victorious with Him over all the enemies of my soul. Blessed Holy Spirit, I pray that You would fill me. Come into my life, break down every idol and cast out every foe. I am thankful, Heavenly Father, for the expression of Your will for my daily life as You have shown me in Your Word. I, therefore, claim all the will of God for today. I am thankful that You have blessed me with all spiritual blessings in heavenly places in Christ Jesus. I am thankful that You have begotten me unto a living hope by the resurrection of Jesus Christ from the dead. I am thankful that You have made a provision so that today I can live filled with the Spirit of God with love and joy and peace, with long-suffering, gentleness and goodness, with meekness, faithfulness, and self-control in my life. I recognize that this is Your will for me and I therefore reject and resist all the endeavors of Satan and his wicked spirits to rob me of the will of God. I refuse in this day to believe my feelings and I hold up *the shield of faith* against all the accusations and distortion and insinuations that Satan would put into my mind. I claim in every way this victory over all satanic forces in my life. I pray in the name of the Lord Jesus Christ with thanksgiving. *Amen.*

— *Victor M. Matthews.*

PRAYER OF A WARRIOR

O, heavenly Father, as the day breaks and I arise this morning, I am aware that I am entering a battlefield. You have given me all of the weapons that I need to prepare for battle and to wage war against the enemy. As I pray in the power of Your Holy Spirit, I claim victory as I put on the armor of God:

First, I put on *the belt of truth* so that as I stand in the truth of your Word; I will not be a victim of Satan's lies.

Next, I put on *the breastplate of righteousness* which is your covering for my shame. I am so grateful that you will not treat me as my sins deserve because Jesus took upon himself the curse of my sin and gave me the gift of this covering in return. Lord, continually change my heart so that more and more, each day, my way of life practically will reflect the way You see me because of Christ.

I now put on *the sandals* that make me ready to stand and advance in the battle. I believe your promise of salvation and because of this, I know that I can have true peace in every circumstance.

I now take up *the shield of faith*. You, O Lord, are my shield. You have given me the power to say "no" to all ungodliness. When I find myself under a great volley of flaming arrows of doubt and deceit, let me find my only security in your power to be my defender.

I place *the helmet of salvation* on my head and I thank you that I am so secure in my salvation that I can look upon the onslaught of the enemy with the full knowledge that I am completely protected by Christ. I thank you, O God, that you have given me a new nature and for the fact that I shall forevermore be under the safety of your command.

Finally, I am grateful for *the sword of the Spirit*, which is Your Word. Teach me to know your Word so that it may be used not only to fend off attacks but also may it be a weapon to strike the adversary with constant and heavy blows.

O Father, by faith I have put on the full armor of God. I am prepared to use these weapons to stand firm against all the attacks of the evil one and to live confidently in the victory already won for me by the Lord Jesus Christ. It is in His name that I pray. *Amen.*

— *Kathryn McBride*

Chapter Two

AFFIRM

*"The major strategy of Satan is to distort the character
of God and the truth of who we are. He can't change God
and he can't do anything to change our identity and position
in Christ. If, however, he can get us to believe a lie,
we will live as though our identity in Christ isn't true.*

— *Dr. Neil T. Anderson*

Affirming My Position in Christ

My great and gracious Heavenly Father, I worship you and praise you for who you are. You are the creator, sustainer, and providential controller of the universe and of my life. You sent your Son, the Lord Jesus to take away our sins. I believe that He is fully God and fully man, without sin, who is the only mediator between God and men; that He lived a sinless life and taught us your truth; that He died in my place to give to You a complete satisfaction for my sins; and that You enabled me to come to Him in faith for the full forgiveness of my sins.

I take my stand in Christ. I believe that the Holy Spirit baptized me into Christ that very moment I first trusted Christ as my Savior. I now stand complete in Christ. By your strong, saving grace, I now have perfect acceptance in the righteousness of Christ. I have perfect access to your throne of grace in any time of need. I have provided authority to carry on the work you have assigned to me, even to face Satan and his demons and to pray and work against them. *Amen.*

— *Dr. C. Fred Dickason*

My Pledge of Allegiance

On the basis of my position in Christ and realizing that all that I am and have is a grace gift from your hand, I yield my whole being, spirit and body, to You as a reasonable and loving response. I choose to submit to your will and way in my life. I stand against the sinful capacity that resides within me and count myself truly dead to sin and genuinely alive to God through my union with Christ. I also count myself as crucified to the world and its lusts and count the world as crucified to me. I believe that Christ died, rose, and was exalted at the right hand of God the Father, far above all angelic beings good and evil. I count myself as raised and seated with Him in the heavenly places far above my enemies, Satan and demons. I stand against these enemies in the righteousness and authority of the risen and exalted Savior.

I declare my position of victory over these enemies, just as Christ stands over them. I choose this day whom I shall serve. I will serve the Lord Jesus Christ and the Triune God. You and You alone, O Triune God, are worthy of worship and praise. You and You alone are worthy of cultivating my life. I commit my entire mind, my emotions, my will, my needs, my hopes, my relationships and my works to you. Work in my life by the Holy Spirit to will and accomplish all your good pleasure. Give me a heart to follow you completely. Keep me in the way of righteousness for your name's sake, and enable me to stand for you and serve you all of my life. I pray this in the name of the Son of God. *Amen.*

— *Dr. C. Fred Dickason*

DAILY SURRENDER

My Father, I want to thank you that Jesus Christ died for me. I thank you that I also died with Christ. I now accept His death on my behalf. In faith, I choose to die to self-will. I surrender every struggle I have with sin into Your hands. I receive Your cleansing and forgiveness and I crown Christ as Lord of my life. I resist Satan. I affirm his defeat at the cross. I accept the truth that his defeat is final and complete and now in faith, I accept what you have provided for me. I receive the fullness of the Spirit and I desire to walk in obedience. In Jesus name, *Amen.*

— *Dr. Erwin W. Lutzer*

TAKING AN INVINCIBLE STANCE

Gracious heavenly Father, I choose to see myself as You see me in the Person of Your Son, the Lord Jesus Christ. I choose to see myself as one invincibly strong and able to do all that is in Your will for me to do. I reject Satan's accusations that I am hopelessly weak and defeated. I accept my present great need as a call to renewed vision of the victory of my Lord. Help me to focus my attention upon the awesome majesty, power, and sovereign greatness of my heavenly Father, who can do anything but fail. Help me to see that in my union with Christ I am more than a conqueror. Let the burden of my trials become an expression of the burden of the Lord. Let that burden be expressed in tears of concern, times of fasting and prayer. I choose not to shrink back from the burden You wish me to carry.

I recognize, Lord, that it is chiefly my own sin and failure that has brought me to this severe trial. I am deeply sorry for my sins *(mention them by name)*. Cleanse me in my Savior's blood. I take back from Satan all ground I have given him by my sins and transgressions. On the authority of the cross I reclaim all of that ground for the Lord Jesus Christ.

Precious Lord Jesus Christ, You have promised never to leave me nor forsake me. I know that is true, and I boldly say, "The Lord is my helper, I will not fear." I resist the devil and his kingdom, steadfast in the faith. I command Satan and his demons to leave me and to go where the Lord Jesus Christ sends them.

Heavenly Father, I accept and choose to enjoy everything inscribed upon the scroll of Your will for me. Thank You that I can do all things through Christ who is my strength. I will do Your will by accepting my responsibility to be strong. I will do through Your strength the things I know to be Your will *(tell Him what they are)*.

Thank You, loving heavenly Father, that through my Lord Jesus Christ You have heard my prayer — and You will make me to walk as one so strong in the Lord that even Satan's most powerful strategies are already defeated. In the name of the Lord Jesus Christ and for Your glory I pray. *Amen.*

— *Dr. Mark I. Bubeck*

THE DAILY AFFIRMATION OF FAITH

Today I deliberately choose to submit myself fully to God as He has made Himself known to me through the Holy Scripture which I honestly accept as the only inspired, infallible, authoritative standard for all life and practice. In this day I will not judge God, His work, myself, or others on the basis of feelings or circumstances.

I recognize by faith that the triune God is worthy of all honor, praise, and worship as the Creator, Sustainer and End of all things. I confess that God, as my Creator, made me for Himself. In this day I, therefore, choose to live for Him *(Revelation 5:9-10; Isaiah 43:1, 7, 21; Revelation 4:11).*

I recognize by faith that God loved me and chose me in Jesus Christ before time began *(Ephesians 1:1-7).*

I recognize by faith that God has proven His love to me in sending His Son to die in my place, in whom every provision has already been made for my past, present, and future needs through His representative work, and that I have been quickened, raised, seated with Jesus Christ in the heavenlies, and anointed with the Holy Spirit *(Romans 5:6-11; 8:28-39; Philippians 1:6-7, 13, 19; Ephesians 1:3; 2:5-6; Acts 2:1-4, 33).*

I recognize by faith that God has accepted me, since I have received Jesus Christ as my Lord and Savior *(John 1:12; Ephesians 1:6);* that He has forgiven me *(Ephesians 1:7)*; adopted me into His family, assuming every responsibility for me *(John 17:11, 17; Ephesians 1:5; Philippians 1:6)*; given me eternal life *(John 3:36; 1 John 5:9-13)*; applied the perfect righteousness of Christ to me so that I am now justified *(Romans 5:1; 8:3-4; 10:4)*; made me complete in Christ *(Colossians 2:10)*; and offers Himself to me as my daily sufficiency through prayer and the decisions of faith *(1 Corinthians 1:30; Colossians 1:27; Galatians 2:20; John 14:13-14; Matthew 21:22; Romans 6:1-19; Hebrews 4:1-3, 11)*.

I recognize by faith that the Holy Spirit has baptized me into the Body of Christ *(1 Corinthians 12:13)*; sealed me *(Ephesians 1:13-14)*; seeks to lead me into a deeper walk with Jesus Christ *(John 14:16-18; 15:26-27; 16:13-15; Romans 8:11-16)*; and to fill my life with Himself *(Ephesians 5:18)*.

I recognize by faith that only God can deal with sin and only God can produce holiness of life. I confess that in my salvation my part was only to receive Him and that He dealt with my sin and saved me.

Now I confess that in order to live a holy life, I can only surrender to his will and receive Him as my sanctification; trusting Him to do whatever may be necessary in my life, without and within, so I may be enabled to live today in purity, freedom, rest and power for His glory *(John 1:12; 1 Corinthians 1:30; 2 Corinthians 9:8; Galatians 2:20; Hebrews 4:9; 1 John 5:4; Jude 24)*.

Having confessed that God is worthy of all praise, that the Scriptures are the only authoritative standard, that only God can deal with sin and produce holiness of life, I again recognize my total dependence upon Him and submission to Him. I accept the truth that praying in faith is absolutely necessary for the realization of the will and grace of God in my daily life *(1 John 5:14-15; James 2:6; 4:2-3; 5:16-18; Philippians 4:6-7; Hebrews 4:1-13; 11:6, 24-28)*.

Recognizing that faith is a total response to God by which the daily provisions the Lord has furnished in Himself are appropriated, I therefore make the following decisions of faith:

For this day *(Hebrews 3:6, 13, 15:4-7)* I make the decision of faith to surrender wholly to the authority of God as He has revealed Himself in the Scripture — to obey Him. I confess my sin, face the sinful reality of my old nature, and deliberately choose to walk in the light, in step with Christ, throughout the hours of this day *(Romans 6:16-20; Philippians 2:12-13; 1 John 1:7, 9).*

For this day I make the decision of faith to surrender wholly to the authority of God as revealed in the Scripture—to believe Him. I accept only His Word as final authority. I now believe that since I have confessed my sin He has forgiven and cleansed me *(1 John 1:9).* I accept at full value His Word of promise to be my sufficiency and rest, and will conduct myself accordingly *(Exodus 33:1, 1 Corinthians 1:30; 2 Corinthians 9:8; Philippians 4:19).*

For this day I make the decision of faith to recognize that God has made every provision so that I may fulfill His will and calling. Therefore, I will not make any excuse for my sin and failure *(1 Thessalonians 5:24).*

For this day I make the decision of faith deliberately to receive from God that provision which He has made for me.

I renounce all self-effort to live the Christian life and to perform God's service; renounce all sinful praying which asks God to change circumstances and people so that I may be more spiritual; renounce all drawing back from the work of the Holy Spirit within and the call of God without; and renounce all non-biblical motives, goals, and activities which serve my sinful pride.

I now sincerely receive Jesus Christ as my sanctification, particularly as my cleansing from the old nature, and ask the Holy Spirit to apply to me the work of Christ accomplished for me in the crucifixion. In cooperation with, and dependence upon Him, I obey the command to "put off the old man" *(Romans 6:1-14; 1 Corinthians 1:30; Galatians 6:14; Ephesians 4:22).*

I now sincerely receive Jesus Christ as my sanctification, particularly as my enablement moment by moment to live above sin, and ask the Holy Spirit to apply to me the work of the resurrection to that I may walk in newness of Life. I confess that only God can deal with my sin and only God can produce holiness and the fruit of the Spirit in my life. In cooperation with, and dependence upon Him, I obey the command to "put on the new man" *(Romans 6:1-4; Ephesians 4:24).*

I now sincerely receive Jesus Christ as my deliverance from Satan and take my position with Him in the heavenlies, asking the Holy Spirit to apply to me the work of the ascension. In His Name I submit myself to God and stand against all of Satan's influence and subtlety. In cooperation with, and dependence upon God, I obey the command to "resist the devil" *(Ephesians 1:20-23; 2:5; 4:27; 6:10-18; Colossians 1:13; Hebrews 2:14-15; James 4:7; 1 Peter 3:22; 5:8-9).*

I now sincerely receive the Holy Spirit as my anointing for every aspect of life and service for today. I fully open my life to Him to fill me afresh in obedience to the command to "be filled with the Holy Spirit" *(Ephesians 5:18; John 7:37-39; 14:16-17; 15:26-27; 16:7-15: Acts 1:8).*

Having made this confession and these decisions of faith, I now receive God's promised rest for this day *(Hebrews 4:1-13).* Therefore, I relax in the trust of faith, knowing that in the moment of temptation, trial, or need, the Lord Himself will be there as my strength and sufficiency *(1 Corinthians 10:13).*

— *Unknown*

Chapter Three

RESIST

"Christ came to set the captive free.
Satan comes to make the free captive.
Christ wants to cut some binding ropes from our lives.
Satan will want to use them to tie us in knots."

— Beth Moore

Resistance to Darkness

Maybe a simple process to follow will help:

- Vocally declare your faith in the Lord Jesus Christ. Use His full title as you do this. Openly acknowledge that He is your Master, your Lord, and the One Who has conquered all other powers at the cross.

- Deny any and all allegiance to the devil his demonic host and the occult. Do this forcefully and boldly. Again, express things aloud.

- Claim the full armor of God, based on Ephesians 6:10-17, as your complete protection. Read the passage orally with emphasis.

- Finally, state firmly your resistance of demonic influence. Consider using the following prayer. Use it as a guide when you begin to feel afraid and sense the attack of evil forces.

I do now renounce any and all allegiance I have ever given to Satan and his host of wicked spirits. I refuse to be influenced or intimidated by them. And, I refuse to be used by them in any way whatsoever. I reject all their attacks upon my body, my spirit, my soul and my mind. I claim the shed blood of the Lord Jesus Christ throughout my being. And I revoke all their power and influence within me or round about me. I resist them in the name of my Lord and Master, Jesus Christ, the Champion over evil. I stand secure in the power of the cross of Calvary whereby Satan and all his powers become defeated foes through the blood of my Lord Jesus Christ. I stand upon the promises of God's Word. In humble faith, I do here and now put on the whole armor of God that enables me to stand firm against the schemes of the devil.

— *From the Booklet, Demonism, by Charles R. Swindoll*

I refuse the *influence* of the enemy.

I refuse to be *led* by the enemy.

I refuse to be *guided* by the enemy.

I refuse to *obey* the enemy.

I refuse to *pray* to the enemy.

I refuse to *ask* anything of the enemy.

I refuse to *surrender* to the enemy.

I refuse all *knowledge* from the enemy.

I refuse to *listen* to the enemy.

I refuse *visions* from the enemy.

I refuse the *touch* of the enemy.

I refuse *messages* from the enemy.

I refuse all *help* from the enemy.

— *Unknown*

A PRAYER OF RESISTANCE

Father, I am your servant: I am committed to Your will and glory. I come to You through my high priest, Jesus Christ, and ask You to expose in the light of Your presence all satanic schemes and enemies of yours that war against me. In the authority of Jesus Christ, with whom I am now seated at Your right hand in the heavenlies, I now resist this attack of Satan: I remove all ground of advantage that you and your forces have taken in my life; and now cover it completely with the blood of Jesus Christ.

I declare broken all power structures of evil, all hierarchies of demonic energy, all schemes ever devised against me for any cause, through any source, at any time. I bind, rebuke and command the departure of all ancestral spirits that have come against me to hinder my effectiveness as a servant of the Lord Jesus Christ. In His name, which is supreme, I command you to leave me now. *Amen.*

— *Unknown*

Roundup Prayer
(Continuing Resistance to Demonic Influence)

I worship and honor my heavenly Father, The Lord Jesus Christ, and the Holy Spirit; the true and living God who promised, "I will never leave you or forsake you." I welcome and honor the unseen presence of my Lord Jesus Christ who promised always to be with us when we meet in His name. I honor and thank You, Lord Jesus Christ, for Your invisible presence in this very place with us. I ask You to be in charge and to effect only Your will and plan in our lives. I yield fully to Your will in the eviction of any and all wicked spirit control from my life. I desire the Holy Spirit to do the sanctifying work within my whole person and being that He is there to accomplish. I ask You, Lord Jesus Christ, to assign Your holy angels to protect us from any strategies of darkness designed to oppose this prayer for freedom. Keep Satan and all his opposing hosts of evil away from us. I also ask You to insure that wicked spirits evicted from my presence will depart quickly and directly to the place to which You consign them.

In the name of my Lord Jesus Christ and by the power of His blood, I affirm my authority over all wicked spirits assigned to control me and hinder my life and my witness for Christ. I now command all lingering wicked spirits assigned to harass, rule and control me to cease their work and be bound in the presence of the Lord Jesus Christ. I bind all backup systems and replacer wicked spirits assigned to rebuild evicted strongholds. They may not do that! I command all those spirits assigned against me to be and remain whole spirits. I forbid any dividing, restructuring, or multiplying of wicked spirits working against me. There is to be one-way traffic of evil spirit activity out of my life and to the place that the Lord Jesus Christ consigns them. I pull in from other family members all those wicked spirits working under the chain of authority established by the powers of darkness assigned to rule over me. I command them all to be bound together here in the presence of my Lord Jesus Christ in that spiritual realm where He dwells with me and they know His presence. It is my will that all powers of darkness having assignment against me must hear and obey Him who is their Creator and Conqueror. I command their full attention to the Lord Jesus Christ, I declare Him to be my Redeemer and Lord. I affirm that God has seated me with Christ Jesus in the heavenly realms far above all principalities and supernatural powers of darkness and evil.

Lord Jesus Christ, I ask You to tell all of these powers of darkness assigned to afflict and rule over me where they must go. I want them out of my life and confined where they can never trouble me again. I yield fully to Your sovereign plan for my life and all of the purposes You have in this battle I have been facing. I ask You, Lord Jesus Christ, to tell them clearly where they must go. *(A brief pause is in order to honor the Lord Jesus Christ's work of addressing His authority and victory against those powers of darkness bound in accountability before Him).* I now ask the Holy Spirit dwelling within my person to effect the will of the Lord Jesus Christ concerning these afflicting powers of darkness. Just as You forced them out of people's lives in response to Jesus' commands when He walked on this earth, I ask You to accomplish that for me now. I ask You, Spirit of the Living God, to evict from my conscious, subconscious, and unconscious mind all control of any wicked powers. Break all their power and manipulation of my thought processes. They must go where the Lord Jesus Christ sends them. Sweep them away and make my mind clear of any wicked spirit dominion. I now ask that the Holy Spirit would renew and sanctify my mind. Cleanse and take full possession of my conscious, unconscious, and subconscious mind, precious Holy Spirit. Set it totally apart for the glory of God and the service of my Lord Jesus Christ. I deliberately yield my mind to the lordship of Christ, the truth of God's Work, and the will of my heavenly Father.

I now ask that the Holy Spirit would look all through my emotions on the conscious, subconscious, and unconscious level. Evict any controlling powers of darkness and may the holy angels escort them to the place where the Lord Jesus Christ is commanding them to go.

Clean them out and take them totally away from my person. I ask that the gracious Holy Spirit would take control of my emotions on every level of the function of my feelings. Sanctify my emotions. Fill my emotions with the Spirit's fruit of love, joy, peace, patience, gentleness, meekness, faithfulness, and self-control. I welcome the Holy Spirit's internal control of my feelings. I look to the Spirit of God to sanctify and renew my emotions. I reach out to experience the Lord's plan for my emotional freedom and spiritual well being.

I now ask that the Holy Spirit would look all through my conscious, unconscious, and subconscious will for any control of wicked powers. Evict them now to where the Lord Jesus Christ is commanding them to go. Sweep my volition totally clean from evil control and manipulation. May the Holy Spirit of the true and living God renew and sanctify my will fully for the glory of God. Will within me to do God's good will. May the lordship of Jesus Christ be obediently lived out in my life by the Holy Spirit's enabling control of my will.

I offer my body in all of its parts and functions as an expression of my spiritual worship to my heavenly Father. I ask the Holy Spirit to look all through my body for any controlling activity of wicked spirits. Look all through my brain and central nervous system for any fallen spirit's affliction or control. Evict them totally away from this physical control center for the function of my mind and body. I offer my brain and its capacities for the quickening, renewing control of the Holy Spirit. Sanctify and refresh my brain so that it functions in spiritual harmony with Your control of my whole person. Look all through my body and sever any wicked spirit control of my senses of vision, hearing, smell, touch, or taste.

Look all through the organs of my body for any defiling work of the kingdom of darkness. Sanctify my body's organs and their functions by the quickening work of the Holy Spirit.

I surrender all my physical appetites to Your Lordship. I give You my need and cravings for food and drink. Examine and cleanse me from demonic activity in all the organs of my digestive system. Set apart my sexuality for the glory of God. Evict any work of the enemy in my sexual functions and organs. I surrender these to Your Lordship, and I submit myself to Your holy plan for moral purity and sexual intimacy only in the bonds of marriage.

Evict any afflicting, evil power totally away from every part of my body. Sanctify it in its entirety. I want my body to be a "holy body," not only in its standing in God's redemptive plan but also in its function. As a part of my spiritual worship to my Father in heaven, I offer my body as a living sacrifice to be used only for all that is acceptable in His sight.

I now yield up my whole person again to the true and living God and His full control. I ask the Father, Son, and the Holy Spirit to control me fully. I thank You for the freedom that You have effected within me during this time of prayer. I now look to the love of my heavenly Father, the lordship of Jesus Christ, and the ministry of the Holy Spirit to enable me to daily walk in the spiritual freedom promised me in God's holy Word. I reject, resist, and refuse anything less. In the name and worthiness of my Lord Jesus Christ and by the intercessions of the Holy Spirit, I place these petitions before my Father in heaven.

— *Dr. Mark I. Bubeck*

CARPENTER'S PRAYER

Dear Heavenly Father I come to acknowledge you as the infinite Sovereign over all creation. I *rejoice* and take refuge in the certainty that you are my God. You dwell in the heavens, and you do whatever pleases you *(Psalm 115:6)*.

I *acknowledge* that your purposes stand forever, and cannot be opposed. By men, angels, principalities, powers or any other creature *(Isaiah 46:10; Romans 8:38-39)*.

I *thank you* that you are a God who loves righteousness and justice, and that the earth is full of your unfailing love *(Psalm 33:5)*.

I *thank you* that you are compassionate and gracious, slow to anger, abounding in love for your people *(Psalm 103:8)*.

I *thank you* that in Christ you have loved me from eternity with a love that surpasses knowledge *(Ephesians 1:4-5; 3:19)*.

I *thank you* that you have forgiven all my sins and transgressions *(Colossians 2:13)*, and have removed them from me as far as the east is from the west *(Psalm 103:12)*.

I *acknowledge* that in your sovereign wisdom You are the Most High God who transforms curse into blessing *(Numbers 23:7-24:10)*, who infallibly brings good out of evil *(Genesis 50:20)*, who takes the crafty in their craftiness *(1 Corinthians 3:19)*, and, in the greatest irony of all, appoints death as the way to life *(Galatians 2:20)*.

I *come* boldly before You this day, solely on the merits of my Savior, Lord, and High Priest, Jesus Christ, the righteous One, to ask you to remove the curses that have been imposed on me in the past, and turn them into the blessings that are mine in Christ.

I *ask* that you would give me the strength to pray this prayer, and I bind all attempts of Satan to interfere with my supplication.

I *ask* that you would, as David prayed, unite my heart, my whole inner self, to praise your name and petition your throne *(Psalm 86:11)*.

Open the entire system of personalities that have been formed by the curses of Satan, and cause them to join in my prayer. Do not allow those personalities which are still in bondage to Satan's lies to interfere. Make them rather to listen quietly as I pray. Do not allow those personalities that have been formed as a habitation for Satan's demons, or the inhabiting demons themselves, to interfere with my petitions. Ordain and appoint for me that I might pray in the energy, power and enablement of the Holy Spirit, whose power as the representative of the living Christ is greater than any power of hell.

I begin by *acknowledging,* as did Jeremiah *(Jeremiah 14:20),* Daniel *(Daniel 9:4-19)* and Nehemiah *(Nehemiah 9:2-37),* and I am linked to the guilt of my ancestors and their rebellion against you.

I *renounce* the sins of my father and mother, and all the ancestors of my past, known and unknown, whose sins in one measure or another have been visited upon me. Through the power of the precious blood of my Lord Jesus Christ, I affirm that I have been redeemed from all the consequences of their empty, unbelieving way of life, transmitted to me in their sins and rebellion against you *(1 Peter 1:18-19).* In the name of the Lord Jesus Christ, I break all strongholds of the powers of darkness because of the sinful ground given by my generational lineage going back three and four generations *(Exodus 20:5).* I claim the death, burial and resurrection of my Lord Jesus Christ as that which sets me free from any and all generational curses, and which alone has the power to reverse and set free both me and my children from all generational transfer of the powers of darkness.

I specifically *renounce* any involvement of my father and mother, and all my ancestors, known and unknown, in false religions, occult practices, witchcraft and Satanism.

I *renounce* ever signing my name over to Satan or having my name signed over to Satan. I announce that my name is written in the Lamb's Book of Life.

I *renounce* any ceremony where I may have been wed to Satan. I announce that I am the bride of Christ.

I *renounce* any and all covenants that I made with Satan. I announce that I am a beneficiary of, and participant in, the New Covenant which has brought me into union with my Lord Jesus Christ.

I *renounce* ever giving of my blood in the service of Satan. I announce that I trust only in the shed blood of my Lord Jesus Christ.

I *renounce* ever eating flesh or drinking blood in Satanic worship, whether acquired from animal or human sacrifice or both. By faith I eat only the flesh and drink only the blood of the Lord Jesus at the supper which He instituted and still hosts in His church.

I *renounce* any ceremonies or rituals that I have participated in to placate or gain the favor and power of Satan. I announce that Jesus alone drank the cup of God's wrath for me, and that through the sacrifice of Christ, all the claims of God's righteousness against my sins have been satisfied, and therefore that I stand fully accepted in the Beloved One, God's only Son.

I *renounce* any and all guardians and Satanic parents that were assigned to me. I announce that God is my Father *(Romans 8:15)*, and that the Lord Jesus Christ is the Shepherd and Guardian of my soul *(1 Peter 2:25)* through the Holy Spirit who indwells me, and by whom I am sealed unto final redemption *(Ephesians 1:13-14)*.

I *renounce* any and all curses that were placed upon me as a part of the worship of Satan. I announce that my Lord Jesus Christ became a curse for me when He was nailed to the cross *(Galatians 3:13)*.

I *reject* all Satanic assignments, programs, and responses that were placed in altars brought into existence to hold me in bondage to Satan and the powers of darkness. I accept only God's assignments and purposes for me in Christ.

I *reject* and bind any and all cultic spirits who have been assigned to hold me in bondage to specific sins, curses or spells, and thereby maintain Satan's continued control in my life.

I *affirm* that I have been transferred from the kingdom of darkness into the kingdom of God's Beloved Son *(Colossians 1:13),* and that I am now the willing servant of my Lord Jesus Christ alone, and I am dedicated to seeking and advancing His kingdom and righteousness *(Romans 6:17-22).*

I *reject* any and all false memories Satan has placed in my mind or the mind of any alters designed to traumatize and hold me in bondage to a false past. I acknowledge that the Lord Jesus Christ and the indwelling Holy Spirit are the custodians of the truth about my past, and they will sovereignly bring to mind those memories through which they intend to bring the gifts of healing and freedom to me.

I *renounce* the work of Satan which has made me a receptacle for demonic power headed by a lead ranking spirit named Death, and by which my life, identity, thoughts, and functioning have been confused and cursed. I announce that by His death, Christ has rendered powerless the one who has the power of death, Satan himself *(Hebrews 2:14)*; that my life is now hidden with Christ in God *(Colossians 3:3)*, and my identity and functioning are based on who I am in Christ.

I *acknowledge* that my own sins, and not just the sins of my ancestors, have contributed to my bondage. I repent of all the sin that Satan has used as ground to expand his power and control in my life. I ask that you would reveal those sins to me, and then deepen my repentance from them, so that the work of the Holy Spirit in forming Christ in me is not hindered *(Galatians 4:19).*

I *bind* all wicked spirits involved in carrying out the curse of Satan against me, and command them to reverse their work. I turn every curse of Satan sent against me back on Satan and all his wicked host, who have been appointed to oversee and carry out those curses against me.

I *acknowledge,* Lord Jesus, that you are my shepherd, and that you prepare a table before me in the presence of my enemies *(Psalm 23:5).* I pray that the table you prepare before my enemies (wicked spirits) will become their snare, retribution and trap. May their eyes be darkened so they cannot see, and their backs are broken forever. Pour out your wrath on them; let your fierce anger overtake them *(Psalm 69:22-24).*

Cast them out of the temple of my body, and consign them to the pit, where they must await the judgment reserved for them. You are the Lord who hears the needy, and you do not despise your captive people *(Psalm 69:33).* You came to set the captives free, and I claim that freedom in your name *(Isaiah 61:1).*

I *pray* with David, "Contend, O Lord, with those who contend with me; fight against those who fight against me. Take up shield and buckler; arise and come to my aid. Draw the spear and javelin against those who pursue me. Say to my soul, 'I am your salvation.' May those who seek my life be disgraced and put to shame; may those who plot my ruin be turned back in dismay. May they be like chaff before the wind, with the angel of the Lord driving them away; may their path be dark and slippery, with the angel of the Lord driving them away; Since they hid their net for me without cause and without cause dug a pit for me may ruin overtake them by surprise—may the net they hid entangle them, may they fall into the pot, to their ruin. Then my soul will rejoice to the Lord and delight in his salvation" *(Psalm 35:1-9).*

O Lord, the ancient enemy of your people has raised himself up as the enemy of my soul. Satan has attempted to devour me with his curses—may those curses be turned to devour him. He loves to pronounce curses—may this love become his judgment and that which he sends be that which he receives back. He wears cursing as his garments of glory. May his curses against me become garments of disgrace which he cannot remove. May this be your payment to my adversary and accuser, O Lord God. Deal with me, O Sovereign Lord, for your name's sake. Out of the goodness of your love deliver me. For I am poor and needy, and my heart is wounded within me. I have been crushed by the assault of my enemy. I am an object of Satan's scorn.

I *repent* of my believing them. Send healing to my divided and fragmented heart, and unite it to fear your name only. Bring oneness, wholeness, and integrity to my whole inner person, by undoing the work of Satan and all the wicked host that has been assigned to me.

I *glory* in nothing but the cross of Christ, by which Satan has been defeated *(1 John 3:8),* all principalities and powers haven been take captive *(Colossians 2:14-15),* the power of sin in my flesh has been rendered powerless *(Romans 6:6-7),* the world has been crucified to me, and I to the world *(Galatians 6:14),* and Christ has become my hope, righteousness and wisdom *(1 Corinthians 1:30).*

"Worthy is the lamb who was slain to receive power and wealth and wisdom and strength and honor and glory and praise!" *(Revelations 5:12).* In the strong name of my Lord Jesus Christ I pray, *Amen.*

— *Stephen Carpenter*

Chapter Four

RENOUNCE

"It is the image of God reflected in you that so enrages hell;
it is this at which the demons hurl their mightiest weapons."

— *William Gurnall*

Renouncing Demonic Strongholds

I come before You in repentance for the strongholds in my life. I invite you to bring to my mind, as I am stilled in Your presence, all of the sins for which I require conviction today. Enable me to repent with a contrite heart and to walk out with that repentance. I rely on You to illuminate my path and to keep me from straying from You. Sin distances me from You, and that is the worst pain of all. In your kindness, show me if there is any offensive way in me, and lead me in the way everlasting. *Amen.*

— *Unknown*

Renouncing Improper Personal Actions

Holy Father, I recognize Your claims upon my mind and body. Therefore, I confess and renounce any personal practice that was a deviation from or transgression of the will of God. Any involvement with drugs, alcohol, illicit sex, mind control techniques, TM, martial arts, psychic healing, new age practices, false religions, cults, or sects, I reject.

I stand against Satan and his demons that would seek to use these practices as inroads, and I claim my freedom in Christ from any control and bondage that might have resulted. Thank You, Lord Jesus, for coming to destroy the works of the devil and his hosts. *Amen.*

— *Dr. C. Fred Dickason*

Renouncing Ancestral Influences

Realizing that the Second Commandment promises to the generational line the blessings of obedient ancestors and the curses of idolatrous and disobedient ancestors. I ask you, Lord Jesus, to break and cancel all the curses and evil effects of the sins of my ancestors. Free me and my family from demonic influences that accompany idolatry and controlling sins.

I may not know what evil or sinful matters my ancestors practiced; but if any of them were involved in any form of idolatry, false religions, witchcraft, Satanism or illicit or immoral behavior that has affected me or my family, I confess that those things are evil and ask you to forgive and cancel their effects upon us. If there were ceremonies, sacrifices or dedications of children made by anyone inside or outside against the family, membership in secret societies, such as Masons, I stand against these and ask you to free me and my family from these influences. *Amen.*

— *Dr. C. Fred Dickason*

Prayer for Cancelling Generational Ground

In the name of my Lord Jesus Christ, I cancel the legal ground surrendered by my _____ *(list specifics of what you know).* Here and now, I renounce any claim that any demons have on me, my children, or any other member of my family because of the sins of any ancestors. In the name of Jesus, I command every evil spirit assigned to me or my family as a result of these sins to leave now and go where the Lord Jesus sends you. *Amen.*

— *Dr. Marcus Warner*

Breaking Curses

Father, in the name of Jesus Christ, I come to You sincerely with a desire to be free from all curses and their results. Lord Jesus, I thank You for saving me and cleansing away my sin at the cross. I confess with my mouth that I belong to You. The devil has no power over me because I am cleansed and covered by Your precious blood.

I now confess all of my sins, known and unknown. I repent of them now in the name of Jesus. I ask You, Lord, to forgive me. I now confess the sins of all of my forefathers. In the name and by the blood of Jesus Christ, I break and renounce the power of every demonic curse that was passed down to me through the sins and actions of others. In the name of Jesus Christ, I break the power and the hold of every curse that came to me through sin, my sins and the sins of my forefathers.

In the name of Jesus Christ, I break the power and hold of every curse that came to me through words spoken. In the name of Jesus Christ, I break the power and hold of every curse that came to me through disobedience — mine or my forefathers.

In the name of Jesus Christ, I now renounce, break, and loose myself and my family from all demonic subjection to my father, mother, grandparents or any other human being, living or dead, who has ever in the past or is now dominating or controlling me or my family in any way contrary to the Word and will of God.

In the name of Jesus Christ, I renounce, break, and loose myself and my family from all psychic heredity, demonic strongholds, psychic power, bondages, bonds of inherited physical or mental illness or curses upon me and my family line as a result of sins, transgressions, iniquities, occult or psychic involvement of any member of my family line, living or dead.

In the name of Jesus Christ, I declare every legal hold and every legal ground of the enemy broken and destroyed. Satan no longer has a legal right to harass my family line through curses. Through the blood of Jesus Christ, I am free.

In the name of Jesus Christ, I command all demonic spirits that entered me through curses to leave me now. Go! In the name of Jesus! I confess that my body, soul, and spirit is the dwelling place of the Spirit of God. I am redeemed, cleansed, sanctified, and justified by the blood of Jesus. Therefore neither Satan nor his demons have any place in me nor power over me because of Jesus. Thank you Jesus for setting me free! *Amen*

— *Unknown*

RENOUNCING PRIDE AND SELF-PROMOTION

Lord Jesus, I thank You that You did not retain all of the glory and privileges that were rightfully yours in heaven but that You became a genuine human and humble servant to do the will of Your Father God. For this God highly honored You and gave You the name above every name in heaven and earth. You deserve honor and glory from all whom you have redeemed. You have redeemed me by your precious blood. I, therefore, humble myself before You that You may gain honor and glory from my life.

I renounce all pride and self-promotion as unfitting to our relationship. I realize that Satan fell through selfish ambition and pride. I don't want to side with the enemy. I humbly acknowledge that I have no good thing in my human resources and that I am unable to do any good apart from your enabling grace. Apart from your saving grace, I deserve the fire of hell. Even now that I am through faith in Christ in your grace, I am an unprofitable servant at my best. But what I am designed to be, I will be by the grace of God. Take my life and make it a trophy of your love and grace. Help me to be your servant and the servant of Christ to others whom You love. I abhor pride and choose humility. I will walk in dedication and determination to honor Christ and serve others. *Amen*

— *Dr. C. Fred Dickason*

RENOUNCING ALL BITTERNESS AND GRUDGES

Holy and gracious Father, I realize that your Word tells us to put away all anger, bitterness, and evil speaking and that we are to forgive grievances we may have against others, just as You have forgiven us in Christ. I recognize that I may not have totally forgiven those who have offended me. I may still retain some bitterness in my heart against them, either family, friends, or opponents. Sometimes I might want to retaliate against them. But I choose to follow your command. I may not receive their apology, but I do forgive any who I think have wronged me by turning my case over to you. I will not retain my anger or thoughts of revenge, but allow You to deal with them properly.

If I am able and it is appropriate, I will seek reconciliation. I realize that may not always be possible or proper, but I seek your direction and enablement. I will not seek to exercise my power by retaining my anger, and I refuse to let bitterness continue. You have warned that if such anger continues, we give opportunity to the devil. I take my stand against the sin of lack of forgiveness. I also take my stand against Satan and ask You to free me from his power exercised because of my sin in this area. If anger seeks to return, I will remind myself before You that I have turned the matter over to You for your adjudication. I realize that long standing hurts don't disappear overnight. Protect me from the enemy's tactics that would continue to remind me and condemn me. I am trusting You to handle my mind and my emotions in these matters. Give me a patient, loving, gracious spirit in my attitudes and dealings with others. *Amen.*

— *Dr. C. Fred Dickason*

RENOUNCING IMPROPER TREATMENT RECEIVED

Loving and gracious Father, if I have been treated suspiciously or improperly by anyone who may have had occult or demonic powers,

I ask you to free me from any evil influence in my life that may have resulted.

I confess and renounce the following: having been hypnotized, being magically healed, allowed my mind to be read, had my astrology chart cast, had my eyes read *(iridology)*, had hands laid on me to receive a special gift *(tongues, prophecy, discernment, power)*. I was wrong to have allowed these things.

If I allowed any improper sexual touch or sexual union outside of marriage, I confess that as a violation of your laws, Holy Father, and a violation of the sanctity of my body, which You have bought for Your holy purpose.

If I have allowed someone to lead me through vows or dedications, as in secret societies, I renounce those vows and ask You to free me from any resulting bondage.

I thank you that You are the designer of life and the provider of all that I need. Forgive me for these matters confessed. I take my stand against the enemy who would take advantage of me through such sins. I trust you to remove the enemy's ground and declare it to be gone. *Amen.*

— *Dr. C. Fred Dickason*

RENOUNCING IMPROPER ATTITUDES

I thank you, my wise and gracious Father, that You created me in Your image so that I am a person who can have fellowship with You—to think, feel and choose with You. Forgive me for thinking improperly of myself or of others also made in your image. This has interfered with personal growth and interpersonal relationships. I confess that poor self-esteem that says I am a "nobody" that should be ignored and rejected. I reject an unhealthy view of my mind or my body that would lead me to mistreat myself or hate myself. In doing so, I hate someone that You love and have bought at the awful price of your Son's death. I accept myself—my person, my mind, my sexuality, my body with all its features—because You have wonderfully designed and fashioned me just as I am, apart from the damage I may have inflicted. I thank you for the way You have made me in every detail.

Forgive me, then, for thinking unfittingly of my person or my body. I reject any thoughts of suicide, any attempts to mistreat myself, any misuse of my body in improper display. If I have allowed depression and self-pity to rule my mind, I confess and reject this as sin. I recognize that there may be reasons for depression that I cannot control. For that, I ask proper help and counsel. But for that which I can control, I give myself to You for strength and healing.

Thank You, Holy Father, for giving me freedom from these improper and degrading thoughts. I trust You to change my attitudes. You are able. *Amen.*
— *Dr. C. Fred Dickason*

RENOUNCING PERSONAL OCCULT PRACTICES

Holy Father, whatever involvement I have had in the occult, I totally and specifically renounce as opposed to your person and commands. I confess that by doing so, I have sought hidden knowledge and secret power. By doing this I judged that You, Your truth, and Your provision was not sufficient for me. I recognize this as a form of rebellion and idolatry and I choose against it.

As for any divination in which I dabbled, I confess and stand against. I reject involvement with any of the following: Ouija board, tarot *(predictive)* cards, palm reading, tea leaf reading, astrology, ESP, predictive dreams, repeated *déjà vu* experiences, visiting psychics or fortune tellers.

If I have practiced magic or sought to control persons or things through "mind control," I confess this, too, and stand against it as sin. Any love or hate magic, any binding or loosing, any hurt or healing ceremonies, any attempts to move objects or control circumstances— all these I reject as contrary to trusting in the true and living God. I confess and renounce fantasy games *(as D&D)*. Whatever contact I have sought with spirits, either the human dead or with guiding spirits, I confess and renounce as trafficking with demons and contrary to the commands of God. Any advantage I may have gained through such acts, I renounce and forsake. If I have listened to mediums or channelors, I reject this practice as rebellion against God, the Creator. If I have gained any advantage through such acts, I refuse to use it or continue in it.

Whatever involvement I have had with witchcraft or Satanism, I confess as wretched sin. I renounce any sacrifice, any dedication, any ceremonies linking me to the gods that such people serve. I ask You, the True and Living God, to cleanse and free me from such connections and control. I declare myself free from these.

Thank you, my Heavenly Father, that you are sufficient for me and that you care for me. I cast all my cares upon You and trust You for all my needs. I admit that I do not have the wisdom or the power to stand on my own. Instead of seeking to overcome my limitations by restoring to sinful practices, I will turn to You, with all my weaknesses, for all of my needs. I will trust You and You alone. Thank you for forgiveness and for removing this ground from the enemy. *Amen.*

— *Dr. C. Fred Dickason*

Renouncing Rebellion

Good and gracious Father, I recognize that rebellion against You originally came from Satan. I also realize that I would rebel against You through my own sinful capacities. I confess and renounce all attitudes and practices of rebellion in my life. I will not allow this Satanic practice and influence to continue in my life. You alone are worthy of praise and trust and obedience. I give myself to You this day and every day for all You have for me—the good, pleasing, and perfect will of God. Work in me to trust and obey. Forgive me for rebellion against all rightly constituted human authority in home, school, church and government. Teach me and help me to submit properly to God-established authorities.

Where I have submitted to improperly constituted authorities, siding with them, participating with them, fearing them, forgive me. I reject submission to false teachers, false religious leaders and false doctrine. I claim the forgiveness and cleansing that You promised on the basis of the blood of Christ. *Amen.*

— *Dr. C. Fred Dickason*

Removing Demonic Influence

Spirit of the living God, I ask You to evict from my conscious, subconscious, and unconscious mind all control of any wicked powers. Break all of their power and manipulation of my thought processes. Sweep them away and make my mind clear of any wicked spirits dominion. Renew and sanctify my mind, Holy Spirit.

I now ask the Holy Spirit to look all through my emotions on the conscious, subconscious, and unconscious levels. Evict any controlling powers of darkness. Gracious Holy Spirit, take control of my emotions.

Fill them with the Spirit's fruit of love, joy, peace, patience, gentleness, meekness, faithfulness and self-control.

I now ask the Holy Spirit to look all through my conscious, unconscious and subconscious will for any control of wicked powers. Evict them now to where the Lord Jesus Christ is commanding them to go. Sweep my violation totally clean from evil control and manipulation.

I offer my body in all of its parts and functions as an expression of my spiritual worship to my Heavenly Father. Holy Spirit, look through all my body for any controlling activity of wicked spirits. I surrender all my physical appetites to Christ's lordship and my sexuality for the glory of God. In the name and worthiness of my Lord Jesus Christ I pray. *Amen.*

—*Dr. Mark I. Bubeck*

Renouncing Demonic Harassment

I worship and honor my Heavenly Father, the Lord Jesus Christ, and the Holy Spirit. I ask You, Lord Jesus, to assign Your holy angels to protect me from any strategies of darkness designed to oppose this prayer for freedom.

In the name of my Lord Jesus Christ and by the power of His blood, I affirm my authority over all wicked spirits assigned to control me and hinder my life and witness for Christ. I now command all lingering wicked spirits to cease their work and be bound in the presence of the Lord Jesus Christ. I also bind all replaced wicked spirits assigned to rebuild evicted strongholds. They may not do that! I command all those spirits assigned against me to remain whole spirits. I forbid any dividing, restructuring or multiplying of wicked spirits working against me.

All powers of darkness having assignment against me must hear and obey Him who is their Creator and Conqueror. I affirm that God has seated me with Christ Jesus in the heavenly realms far above all principalities and supernatural powers of darkness.

Lord Jesus Christ, I ask You to tell all of these powers of darkness assigned to rule over me where they must go. Confine them where they can never trouble me again. I yield fully to all of the purposes You have in this battle I have been facing. In Your great name I pray. *Amen.*

—*Dr. Mark I. Bubeck*

PRAYER FOR EVICTING DEMONS

(Having removed all legal ground the Enemy may claim) In the name of my Lord Jesus Christ and by the power of His blood, I bind together as one every demon assigned to me because of this sin, and command them all to leave. Lord Jesus, I ask you to send them where they will trouble me no more and to do whatever is necessary to enforce this eviction. *Amen.*

— *Dr. Marcus Warner*

RENOUNCING DOUBT AND FEAR

Since You are thoroughly and forever trustworthy, O Living God, I renounce doubt and fear as incompatible with our relationship established by You upon my faith in the crucified, risen and exalted Lord Jesus, the Messiah. You have told us not to be anxious, for You care for us intimately and constantly. I would continually cast all my concerns upon You, for You always are concerned about me. Forgive me for fear and anxiety, and teach your weak and failing child to trust in You always.

Forgive me for doubting your love, your care, and your Word in the Scriptures. You have given us all that we need for life and godliness in this present world. Doubt has led me astray to seek other than your best for my life—in jobs, relationships, achievements and pleasures. I reject trusting in myself, my resources, my plans, my friends instead of trusting in my all-powerful Father. Nothing can separate me from your love—neither death nor life, Satan nor demons, things present nor future, height nor depth, time nor space, nor any created thing. I am yours forever, and You are mine. *Amen.*

— *Dr. C. Fred Dickason*

RENOUNCING FEAR

Father, help me to agree with You that I am not subject to fear, but am a child of Your love.

I *reject* fear of the future, for I believe that the future is in Your hands.

I *reject* fear of evildoers, for Your Word says, "Though an army encamp against me, my heart shall not fear; though war arise against me, yet I will be confident…For He will hide me in His shelter in the day of trouble; He will conceal me under the cover of His tent; He will lift me high upon a rock."

I *renounce* fear of rejection, for David wrote in Your Holy Word, "For my father and mother have forsaken me, but the Lord will take me in."

I *renounce* fear of witnessing about Christ, because as Your Word warns, "The fear of man brings a snare." Therefore, I choose to fear You more than I do any human being. I affirm, "The Lord is on my side, I will not fear. What can man do to me?"

I *renounce* the fear of losing my property and possessions, for Your Word says, "I have learned in whatever situation I am, to be content... I know the secret of facing plenty and hunger, abundance and need; I can do all things through Christ who strengthens me."

I *renounce* fear of Satan, for Your Word says he has already been conquered "by the blood of the Lamb and the word of our testimony."

I *renounce* fear of saying "goodbye" to a terminally ill loved one, for Jesus promised, "Let not your heart be troubled...In my Father's house are many rooms; I go and prepare a place for you and if I go and prepare a place for you, I will come again and will take you to myself that where I am you may be also."

I *renounce* fear of death, for I affirm with the Apostle Paul, "For me to live is Christ and to die is gain." Thank You for the promise, "Death is swallowed up in Victory."

I *renounce* fear of martyrdom, for Your Word declares, "Do not fear those who are able to kill the body, but fear Him rather who is able to destroy both soul and body in hell."

I *renounce* fear of loneliness, for we are promised, "Our fellowship is with the Father and with His Son Jesus Christ." And also, "I will never leave you nor forsake you." And again, "Peace I leave with you; my peace I give to you. Not as the world gives do I give to you. Let not your hearts be troubled, neither let them be afraid."

I *renounce* fear of intimidation, for Jesus said, "If the world hates you, know that it has hated me before it hated you. In the world you will have tribulation, but take heart; I have overcome the world."

I *renounce* fear of false accusations. I accept this promise, "Blessed are you when others revile you and persecute you and utter all kinds of evil against you falsely on my account. Rejoice and be glad, for your reward is great in heaven, for so they persecuted the prophets who were before you."

I *renounce* fear of being treated unjustly, for of Jesus we read that, "When He was reviled, He did not revile in return, when he suffered, He did not threaten but continued entrusting Himself to Him who judges justly."

I *renounce* fear of radical Islam and its desire to intimidate us.

I *renounce* fear of political correctness.

I *declare* that "The truth shall set me free," and I choose to live as a free person in Christ Jesus. I shall speak and not be silent.

I *renounce* fear of curses, either known or unknown, spoken against me and my family.

I *renounce* fear of manipulation and control.

I *renounce* fear of being involved in public or political activity.

I *declare* that Jesus Christ is Lord of all.

I *submit* to Jesus as Lord of every area of my life. Jesus Christ is Lord of my home. Jesus Christ is Lord of my relationships. Jesus Christ is Lord of my city. Jesus Christ is Lord of my nation. Jesus Christ is Lord, above all false gods and religions. Jesus Christ is Lord over all the nations of the earth.

I *commit* myself to be a living witness to Jesus Christ as Lord. I am not ashamed of His cross. "God forbid that I should glory except in the cross of Christ."

I *ask* now that You will fill me with Your Holy Spirit, and pour upon me all the blessings of the Kingdom of Jesus Christ.

Grant me the grace to understand the truth of Your Word clearly, and to apply it in every area of my life. Give me words of hope and life, as You promised. Open and bless my lips so that I can speak to others with authority and power in Jesus' name. Give me the boldness to be a faithful witness for Christ. Give me a love for all people, and a passion to share the love of Christ with them.

Grant that I shall carry Your cross as a badge of honor. In Jesus' name, *Amen.*

— *Adapted by Erwin Lutzer from a prayer written by Mark Durie*

RENOUNCING DECEPTION AND SEEKING TRUTH

Dear Heavenly Father, Your word tells me that You desire truth in my inner being. You will cause me to know wisdom and have understanding. Your word, also tells me that the heart of a person is deceitful and I may not always understand or know what is going on in my heart, my innermost being. I now make a decision to have You reveal to me the hidden motives and secrets of my heart. Jesus said, "Satan is the father of lies and a deceiver who is always trying to deceive me into believing lies." At times, I have believed Satan's lies and deceived myself by avoiding the truth and being in denial. In the past, I was hurt, rejected, betrayed, made powerless or abused. At times, I may have made a choice to live in a fantasy world to escape pain or loneliness. This fantasy world was a deception that I believed to escape painful reality. Other times, I chose to forget, to suppress, to split or mentally separate myself from the painful memories or events. These past hurts were more than I could bear. So I buried or forgot them with all of the anger, unforgiveness and vows made against myself and others. I understand that this is part of my life story and by denying their reality, I deny a part of myself. These vows and unforgiveness are giving the enemy an entranceway into my life and body and a spiritual, legal right to harass, afflict, control or drive me in compulsive, ungodly ways.

I now reject this false life and choose to live in truth and in the light. I choose NOT to live in a myth or lie concerning my past. With God's help, I will work on these hurts, unforgiveness and vows, and come to know myself. I do not want these vows coming upon me or others. I now make a choice to turn from this hidden life and close all these doorways in Jesus' name. I take authority in Jesus' name and I rebuke and command all deceiving spirits to leave me now. I know that You, Father, are a discerner of the heart. I ask You to reveal to me the nature of these hidden hurts, pain, anger, vows, lies or sins in my life. I now choose to face the truth and NOT live in denial. I acknowledge that I cannot do this in my own strength. I look to You, Jesus, for Your help in my healing and deliverance. I ask You to search me, O God and know my heart, test me and know my anxious thoughts. See if there is any offensive way in me and lead me in thy way everlasting. *Amen.*

— *Unknown*

Chapter Five

SOUL TIES

*"It is in the midst of anguish and terror that we realise
who God is and the marvel of what He can do."*

— *Oswald Chambers*

Prayers for Breaking Soul Ties

In the name of my Lord Jesus Christ I renounce any soul tie(s) that has been formed between me and _____ through my_____. I cancel any demonic bond that keeps us connected and command those demons to leave now and go where the Lord Jesus sends you. *Amen.*

— *Dr. Marcus Warner*

Process for Breaking Unhealthy/ Sinful Soul-Ties

Prayer for God's Revealing Negative Soul-Ties

Father, I desire to be free from every negative soul-tie in my life. Please reveal and bring to my mind those relationships that have negative and unhealthy soul-ties that need to be severed. Thank you for your desire to see me completely free from the chains of the enemy. I pray this in the name of the true and living Lord Jesus Christ. *Amen.*

Prayer for Forgiveness

Father, I choose to forgive _____ for *(what the issue of the soul-tie is anchored to),* which made me feel *(describe how it made you feel, even if painful, or the feeling attached to the issue.)*

Prayer for each Negative Soul-Tie

Father, I ask you to cancel, sever and completely break all negative relationships established by the forces of darkness between _____ and myself. I renounce in the name and authority of Jesus any tie to _____ empowered by Satan and his evil spirits. I join my Lord Jesus Christ, asking Him to completely destroy all the ungodly, destructive and hurtful effects this relationship has had upon me, my family, my marriage, and my ministry.

Prayer for Taking Back Surrendered Ground

I take back the ground I surrendered in *(unforgiveness and/or this area of negative soul-ties)* with _____; asking, you Father, to tear down the strongholds built by the enemy on this ground and to sweep away all of the debris. I ask you to cover this ground in the cleansing blood of the Lord Jesus Christ, taking back ownership of what you have purchased and rightly own.

By the authority I have in the true and living Lord Jesus Christ, I command any evil spirits or evil entities attached to this ground I just reclaimed or stronghold just destroyed, to leave me now and go, escorted by God's holy angels, to the place where the Lord Jesus Christ would send you. In the name of the Lord Jesus Christ I pray. *Amen.*

Closing Prayer for Negative Soul-Ties

Heavenly Father, I now confess to you all actions I have taken that have led to these negative soul-ties in my life. I thank you for your entire forgiveness that I have in Christ. I now ask you to seal these entryways to my body, soul and spirit. I ask you to restore and heal my soul. I ask for your wisdom and discernment from ever stepping into relationships that would allow the negative soul-ties to be formed again in my life with anyone. I claim the blessing of the Lord Jesus Christ on any part of a soul-tie that is empowered by God. I forbid the enemy of my soul to continue to interfere or make any further use of these relationships against me by the mighty power and authority of Jesus Christ, my Savior and Lord. In His name, the name above all names, the King of Kings, the Lord of Lords, Jesus Christ. *Amen.*

— *Unknown*

Chapter Six

PRAYERS FOR MYSELF

"The primary battle is between the kingdom of darkness and the kingdom of God, between the Antichrist and the Christ, between the father of lies and the Spirit of truth; and we are in that battle whether we like it or not. The primary location of that battle is our minds. Either we believe the lies that keep us in bondage or we believe the truth that sets us free.

— *Dr. Neil T. Anderson, Timothy M. Warner,
"The Beginner's Guide to Spiritual Warfare"*

PRAYER FOR SPIRITUAL VICTORY

Dear Heavenly Father, I praise You that I am united with the Lord Jesus Christ in all of His life and work. By faith I desire to enter into the victory of the incarnation of my Lord today. I invite Him to live His victory in me. Thank You, Lord Jesus Christ, that You experienced all temptations that I experience and yet never sinned.

I enter by faith into the mighty work of the crucifixion of my Lord. Thank You, dear Father, that through Jesus' blood there is a moment-by-moment cleansing from sin, permitting me to fellowship with You. Thank You that the work of the Cross brings Satan's work to nothing.

I enter by faith into the full power and authority of my Lord's resurrection. I desire to walk in the newness of life that is mine through my Lord's resurrection. Lead me into a deeper understanding of the power of the Resurrection.

By faith I enter into my union with the Lord Jesus Christ in His ascension. I rejoice that my Lord displayed openly His victory over all powers as He ascended into glory through the very realm of the prince of the power of the air.

I enter into my victory aggressively and claim my place as more than a conqueror through Him who loves me. I offer up this prayer in the name of the Lord Jesus with thanksgiving. *Amen.*

—*Dr. Mark I. Bubeck*

CENTERED ON GOD

Loving heavenly Father, enable me to keep all things within the perspective of Your sovereignty. Grant to me the wisdom to know that the fierceness of the battle is not evidence of defeat. Help me to thank and praise You for Your purpose in each phase of the battle. I reject all of Satan's purpose for his attack upon me, but I accept all of Your sovereign plan and purpose. I thank You for what You are doing by allowing Satan's kingdom to war against me. Use the battle to refine, to deepen, to mature, to humble, and to build my faith.

Grant to me the insight and understanding to know my victory. I desire that the roots of my assurance of victory would go down deeply into the essential doctrines of Your Word. I want to see myself as being invincibly strong through my union with Christ, the Person and work of the Holy Spirit, the wholeness of Your provided armor, and the allness of prayer. Teach me how to appropriate my victory in a practical, daily practice. These things I ask in the name of my Lord Jesus Christ. *Amen.*

—*Dr. Mark I. Bubeck*

PRAYER FOR JOY AND REST

Heavenly Father, I praise You that You have created humans to be creatures of joy and rest. I ask that You be at work in my system to prepare me to receive those blessings. Every good thing comes from You, and I rely on You to bring those aspects of my creation into my life.

Please arrange relationships for me that give joy and show me how to build joy. Increase my joy strength, Lord, so that I am able to face my life, both past and present, with the capacity to walk in Your footsteps. Help me to allow the rhythm of joy and rest that You intend for me.

Please bring into my life, also, people who can teach me how to enter the rest that my body, mind and heart require. Help me to allow times of quiet together with those people, which will in turn quiet my soul, bring me to rest, and teach me how to quiet myself. You provide strength through rest, and I desire that strength so that every fruit of the spirit is produced in me, and so that I may witness the healing and redemption of every moment of suffering, sin or lostness in my life. Thank You, Lord. *Amen.*

— *Unknown*

Prayer to Live by the Spirit

Blessed Heavenly Father, in the name of the Lord Jesus Christ I desire to walk in the Spirit today. I recognize that only as He manifests the life of Jesus Christ in me will I be able to escape the works of my flesh. I pray that the Holy Spirit may produce His fruit within my whole being and shed abroad in my heart great love for the Heavenly Father, for the Lord Jesus Christ and for others about me.

Forgive me dear Holy Spirit, for the many times I have grieved You by my sinning. Grant to me always the awareness of my sins that I might quickly confess them to God. Grant me also the desire to obey God's precious Word, Grant me discernment to avoid being deceived by false spirits.

I desire that the Holy Spirit fill all my being with His presence and control me by faith. Fill me, Heavenly Father, with His power that You might be glorified through the invincible strength You provide me to do Your will. I trust my victory over the flesh today completely into the hands of the Holy Spirit as I let Him take control of me.

All of this I ask in the name of the Lord Jesus Christ for Your glory. *Amen.*

—*Dr. Mark I. Bubeck*

PRAYER FOR FORGIVENESS

Dear Heavenly Father, I thank You for Your love and kindness toward me. It is Your kindness that has led me to repentance, turning from all my sinful ways, and turning to You. I admit that I have not been kind, patient, and loving to others when they have offended me. I have allowed bitterness and resentment to grow in me, separating me from others and You, Father. At times, I have forgotten this unforgiveness in my heart. This unforgiveness festers deep within me, at times beyond my conscious reach. This affects every aspect of my life and gives the enemy a right to torment me as stated in Matthew 18. I confess that this unforgiveness and bitterness is affecting my life and relationships today. Because of these past hurts, I acknowledge the inability to love or trust others to any depth. I understand that forgiveness is not an emotion but an act of my will. I now choose to exercise my will to forgive others as You, Father have forgiven me. Father, know that You are a searcher of the heart. I ask You to search my heart. Reveal to me any hidden and secret unforgiveness or bitterness toward others that have hurt or offended me. I choose not to be ruled by a spirit of bitterness. I choose to forgive and have a spirit of peace and love in my heart. I repent, forgive and release these people right now. I ask You Heavenly Father, to forgive me and restore me as I forgive those who have offended me.

Jesus promised that the Holy Spirit would bring everything to our remembrance. Dear Holy Spirit, I am asking You to bring to my remembrance anyone I have to forgive and I will forgive them in Jesus' name. *Amen.*

— *Unknown*

Prayer of Repentance

Loving Heavenly Father, I come again to worship You in the wonder of who You are. I confess my sins to You, dear Heavenly Father. Wash me clean in my Savior's precious blood from all that offends You. I recognize within my person a fleshly nature that can be rebellious in Your sight. I affirm that in my union with Christ in His death I am dead to the rule of the fleshly nature.

I desire the new nature You have placed within me to be in charge through the power of my Savior's resurrection. Thank You for having made this new creation in righteousness and true holiness, so I can love You deeply and serve You fully. May Your Holy Spirit enable me to manifest before You and others the fruit of His full control.

I confess that, as a believer, I show my poor, blind and naked condition. Thank You that my Lord Jesus Christ has invited me to come and buy from Him gold refined in His disciplining fires. I want that gold for myself and for Your church. Anoint our eyes with the eye salve that enables us to see things as our Lord Jesus Christ sees them.

I base every request on the merit of our Lord Jesus Christ's finished work. *Amen.*

—*Dr. Mark I. Bubeck*

Prayer Against Temptation

The fleshly desires are part of our lives as believers, but they need not control us. Through prayer, we can apply three biblical steps to freedom from fleshly desires.

First: honest admission and confession of temptation (*Colossians 1:5-10*). Lord Jesus Christ my old fleshly nature is tempting me _____ *(name the temptation, e.g., lust, anger, gossip),* and I know that if it's left to itself, it is wicked enough to cause me to sin against You.

Second: the realization that we have died with Christ *(Romans 6:11; Galatians 5:24).* We should "count [ourselves] dead to sin but alive to God in Christ Jesus." Acknowledge this truth to Christ in prayer. Lord Jesus Christ, I affirm that through the work of Your cross I am dead to my sin nature and ask You to rule and control my flesh and its desire toward _____ *(name of fleshly temptation being experienced at that moment, e.g., anger, lust).*

Third: living in the control of the Holy Spirit *(Galatians 5:16-26).* This requires that we turn to the Holy Spirit: Blessed Holy Spirit, I ask You now to replace this fleshly desire that is tempting me toward _____ *(state the fleshly appeal: e.g., jealousy, lust)* with the fruit of Your control. Put within my mind, will, and emotions Your love, joy, peace, patience and all the virtues that my Lord Jesus Christ enables me to live out for His glory. *Amen.*

—*Dr. Mark I. Bubeck*

PRAYER FOR PHYSICAL HEALING
Recognizing Spiritual Warfare

Heavenly Father, Ruler of ALL, I commit my physical, emotional and spiritual welfare to You for your healing and protection. Please intervene specifically on my behalf to break the power of this disease I am battling. If it is natural, I trust you to personally and directly touch me with the healing I need. If the enemy is taking advantage of this to further the disease or to torture me with the disease, I ask you to break his power and activity along this line and in any way he would seek to oppose my healing. If he had any part in originating this disease, I ask you to judge him directly and severely and to undo any damage he has accomplished. I confess any fear that keeps me from trusting you. I come against discouragement, depression and despair in the name of the Risen Savior and I ask you to encourage my heart and mind. I cancel whatever ground the enemy thinks he has and I command him in the authority of Christ to leave me and to go where Jesus sends him. If there is any part of me hurting and confused because of trauma experienced, I ask You, Heavenly Father, to comfort and heal that part or those parts and to invite them to come to You for your healing. Break any curse or program designed to ruin me, to disable me, or to harm me in any way and set Your protective guard about me to keep from further damage or affliction. I am your child, and You are my God; and I am trusting you to answer me and to show yourself powerful and sufficient for my needs and that of my family. I pray in the name of the Risen Jesus and for the glory of His name.

— *Dr. C. Fred Dickason*

Protection from Wolves in Sheep's Clothing

Dear Heavenly Father, you have warned us that we should beware of those who come in sheep's clothing, but inwardly are ravenous wolves. You have said that in the last days, evil will abound and Satan will clothe himself as an angel of light. Help me, O God, to be filled with love for the truth and avoid the spirit of lies and all falsehood and errors. Help me to recognize and flee from evil so that I may not be moved, but will continue to remain steadfast to the end. May I never be led astray through deceiving powers or false signs and miracles. Protect me from rebellious spirits and the ravenous wolves, those false teachers who have no mercy on your flock. Keep me safe from the enemy, who comes to kill, steal and destroy. O Lord, You are the Great Shepherd, make me so familiar with Your voice that I hear You when You call. Give me the strength to flee temptation and walk in uprightness as I await the day when You, my Savior, shall appear. *Amen.*

— *Kathryn McBride*

Moral Issues

Dear Heavenly Father, Your word tells me in Galatians 5:17, that my flesh lusts or wars against my spirit and I am not to gratify the lusts of my flesh. I put on the Lord Jesus Christ. I will walk by the guidance of the Holy Spirit. Father, You know at times, I struggle with the temptation to gratify the desires of my flesh. I understand that lust is saying, "I must have this at once." Much of this battle is in my mind and thought life. Because of my loneliness and inner pain at times, I may have entertained lustful fantasies in my mind and thoughts. This only increased the desire to gratify my flesh. At times, this battle has been more than I could stand and I have given into the lust of my flesh. I ask You, Father, reveal to me any ways in which I have broken your moral laws.

Father, I am truly sorry. I repent and ask You to forgive me. I acknowledge that all my sins are forgiven in Christ. I repent and cancel all access to my life by evil spirits. I claim the blood of Jesus over me as my protection. I command all evil spirits that have entered my body or mind, to leave me now in Jesus' name. I now make a new commitment to guard my eyes and take every thought captive in obedience to Christ. I will walk by the guidance of the Holy Spirit. I will work to take control of my body and renew my mind, not giving into fleshly lusts. I will depend on the Holy Spirit to help me accomplish this, in Jesus' name. *Amen.*

— *Unknown*

Prayer For Protection

Praise be to You, O God, Our Father, who through your compassion has been my shield against the fiery darts of Satan. You, O Lord, are gracious and merciful. I ask that you forgive me for all that I have done against you today, in thought, word or deed. Turn your mercy towards me that I may find rest this night. May I never turn from you, O God. Grant me your protection as I travel through this life so that the enemy's schemes may never succeed. Lord, You are my light and my salvation, whom shall I fear? You are my strength and my shield, of whom shall I be afraid? My soul clings to you as you defend me. Your right hand keeps me from stumbling. My heart trusts in You and I am helped. You gladden my heart and in the shadow of your wings, I will take refuge. Lord, I cry out to you and you answer my prayers. You are an ever-present help in trouble, therefore, I will not fear. I meditate on your words and they guide me and bring me peace, therefore, I will rejoice. When darkness comes over me, then, Lord, you are the light on my path. *Amen.*

— *Kathryn McBride*

Prayer to Know and Speak Truth

In the name of the Lord Jesus Christ I claim the protection of the **belt of truth**, described in Ephesians 6:14. I pray its protection over my personal life, my home and family, and the ministry God has appointed for my life. I use the **belt of truth** directly against Satan and his Kingdom of darkness. I embrace Him who is the truth, the Lord Jesus Christ, as my strength and protection from all of Satan's deceptions.

I desire that the truth of God's word shall constantly gain a deeper place in my life. I pray that the truth of the word of God may be my heart's delight to study and memorize.

Forgive me for my sins of not speaking the truth. Show me any way in which I am being deceived.

I ask the Holy Spirit to warn me before I deceive anyone and to protect me always from believing Satan's lies. Thank You, Lord, for making my local church a pillar and foundation for Your truth in my life. Help me to relate to my church and give protection to others as well as receive it myself.

I see, Lord Jesus Christ that my ability to be strong and to do Your will requires the stabilizing power of the *belt of truth*. Thank You for providing this part of the armor. *Amen.*

—Dr. Mark I. Bubeck

PRAYER FOR CONFESSING AND CANCELLING SIN

Lord Jesus Christ, I confess that I have been involved in_____. Please forgive me for this sin and misuse of my body and cancel any ground that the Enemy may claim because of this sin. I choose now to receive your forgiveness and in so doing to forgive myself, so that I will not remain in bondage to this sin any longer. *Amen.*

— Dr. Marcus Warner

GENERAL WARFARE

Heavenly Father, I come to You in the name of Your Son, Jesus, who was born in the flesh approximately 2000 years ago, led a sinless, holy life, suffered and died on the cross and rose again to life to conquer sin and death. It is to You and You alone that I pray. I choose to forgive all human vessels as sources of this warfare. I pray blessings on all human vessels and through this forgiveness, I ask, Lord, that You would also have mercy on those who You would have mercy, and bring salvation and redemption back into the human sources from where those attacks originate.

Lord, I ask that You would allow me to repent for all sins that built up this demonic power, including past generational sins committed and sins committed in this generation. Lord, if there are specific sins You would have me repent on behalf of any person or persons, please bring these to mind and I will confess them. Lord, I ask that You expose the enemy and all his strongholds, and reduce his power for every moment this attack continues until the enemy's strongholds are defeated. Please give me the grace that is sufficient to endure whatever You would call me to endure for Your namesake.

May Your kingdom increase as You turn everything that is meant for evil into good for Your glory. I ask that this prayer remain before Your throne, increasing in authority until You have accomplished all You want to do through this prayer. *Amen.*

— *Unknown*

How to Respond to Intense Struggles with Satan

First: express positive faith toward the Lord: "In the name of the Lord Jesus Christ, I accept every purpose my Lord has for allowing me to experience this fierce battle with Satan. I desire to profit and to learn all of my Lord's purpose in this battle."

Second: in negative rejection of Satan's purpose: "In the name of the Lord Jesus Christ and by the power of His blood I reject every purpose of Satan and His kingdom in afflicting me in this battle. I command every wicked spirit behind this affliction to leave my presence and to go where the Lord Jesus Christ sends him." *Amen.*

— *Unknown*

COMING AGAINST THE ENEMY

Loving heavenly Father, You are the stronghold of my life; of whom shall I be afraid? I worship You and love You for being omnipotent, almighty, and absolute in Your transcendent greatness and unequaled power. Thank You that, no matter how formidable and threatening the forces of darkness become, those who are with us are always "more" than those who are with them. I affirm that Your almightiness is unapproachable by any challenger and that Your power is full of glory.

I worship You, heavenly Father, in the worthy merit of the Lord Jesus Christ. I affirm that He is Lord to the glory of God the Father. I hold all of His person and work directly upon my life as my protection during this time of prayer. I choose to abide in His incarnation, His cross, His resurrection, His ascension, and His glorification.

I come in humble obedience to use the weapons of my warfare against the darkness that is seeking to rule the people of my city, country, and world. I affirm that the weapons You have given me to use are filled with divine power that is sufficient to demolish every stronghold Satan has built to hold back Your will and plan.

I confess the awful wickedness and sins that I, my family, my fellow believers, and my culture have committed. Wash me afresh in the blood of my Lord Jesus Christ that there may be no hindrance to Your fellowship and blessing upon me. I apologize to You for the offense against You represented in the wicked sins characterizing our culture. I recognize that when people abandon themselves in such sinful rebellion, much ground is being given to Satan to rule in our culture. My only hope is knowing that the finished work of my Lord Jesus Christ is sufficient payment for even these. I ask you to bring about all that is necessary to grant us the gift of repentance and a broken humility before You. I invite You to draw near to the people of our day until we are humbled and broken before You in a revival awakening greater than any that has ever been.

In the mighty name of my Lord Jesus Christ, I use the weapons of my warfare to demolish and weaken every throne, dominion, princely ruler, authority, power of darkness, and wicked spirit in the heavenly realm that is organized and strategized to hinder revival. I ask the Holy Spirit to hold the mighty power of the shed blood and finished work of my Lord Jesus Christ constantly against these strongholds to cause their destruction and defeat.

In the name of the Lord Jesus Christ and by the power of His blood, I pull down all levels of the stronghold of _____.
(Choose items from the following list of areas of Satan's strongholds that you desire to pull down and smash. You may think of other things — the list is suggestive, not exhaustive.)

Pornography
Perverted sexual practices
Adultery and prostitution
Drug use and promotion
Alcohol addiction
Abortion practices and promotion
Unbelief and humanism
Neo-pagan teaching
Occult promotion and activity
Satan worship
Television and media distortions
Religious cults and isms (name those you know)
Liberal theology and false doctrines
Divisive influences in the body of Christ
Violence and abuse
Child abuse in all its forms
Divorce and family disunity
Materialism and greed
Peer pressure
Spiritual deafness and spiritual blindness

Blocking of people from sharing their faith
Blocking of people from receiving Christ
Lack of care for the homeless and hurting
Disunity and distrust in Christ's body
Attacks on pastors, Christian workers, and their families
Interest in spiritism and evil supernaturalism
Promotion of hate, rage and violent anger
Hindrance of the recruitment and funding of missionaries
Pride, spiritual haughtiness, and indifference
Neglect of Bible study and prayer

I pull down these strongholds in the name of my Lord Jesus Christ, and I pray their wicked work back upon themselves. I ask my loving Father in heaven to assign His holy angels to engage in direct combative defeat of these strongholds of evil. I bind the work of evil powers in each of these strongholds, and I invite the Holy Spirit to unleash His mighty, convicting power upon the people who are in bondage to them.

I ask Him to exalt the ways of righteousness before the spiritual understanding of such people and to convict them deeply of their accountability to God in coming judgment. I ask the Holy Spirit to open their spiritual eyes to see their need for the saving grace of our Lord Jesus Christ. May this revival for which I pray bring multitudes into a saving relationship with Him.

I address my prayer against the strongholds assigned to keep God's people from believing You for revival awakening. Surely there must be many who are working to make Your people lukewarm and satisfied with our materialism and blind to our spiritual needs. I pull down all such strongholds, named and unnamed, and I pray for a great moving of the Holy Spirit to bring to us a hungering and a thirsting after righteousness. May the Holy Spirit arouse in Christ's body an insatiable appetite to memorize, study, and know God's Holy Word.

In the name of my Lord Jesus Christ I plead for a revolutionary revival to visit my heart, my family, my church, and the whole body of Christ until it spills over upon the world around us and brings many souls into glory. *Amen.*

—*Dr. Mark I. Bubeck*

Chapter Seven

PRAYERS FOR OTHERS

"No picture of the Christian life is more frequently cited than that of a soldier engaging in mortal combat. The idea of Christians standing clothed in full armor has captured the mind and heart of every generation. All believers instinctively understand that they are called to fight — to be good soldiers, to put on their armor, to take up their weapons of righteousness, to enter the fray unafraid, to stand against the fierce assault of evil, and having done all, to stand victorious at the end of the day. Adopting a warfare mentality means understanding that we are always at war, that a battle is raging all around us, and that we ourselves are frontline soldiers. In this battle we fight a foe that is invisible to us, and for that reason it is easy to forget that there is a battle at all until the attack suddenly comes."

— Dr. Ray Pritchard

PRAYER FOR A FRIEND IN BONDAGE

Heavenly Father, I bring before You and the Lord Jesus Christ one who is very dear to You and me, _____. I have come to see that Satan is blinding and binding him/her in awful bondage. He/she is in such a condition that he/she cannot or will not come to You for help on his/her own. I stand in for him/her in intercessory prayer before Your throne. I draw upon the Person of the Holy Spirit that He may guide me to pray in wisdom, power, and understanding.

In the name of the Lord Jesus Christ, I loose _____ from the awful bondage the powers of darkness are putting upon him/her. I bind all powers of darkness set on destroying his/her life. I bind them aside in the name of the Lord Jesus Christ and forbid them to work. I bind up all powers of depression that are seeking to cut _____ off and imprison him/her in a tomb of despondency. I bring in prayer the focus of the Person and work of the Lord Jesus Christ directly upon _____ to his/her strengthening and help. I bring the mighty power of my Lord's incarnation, crucifixion, resurrection, ascension and glorification directly against all forces of darkness seeking to destroy him/her. I ask the Holy Spirit to apply all of the mighty work of the Lord Jesus Christ directly against all forces seeking to destroy _____.

I pray, heavenly Father, that You may open _____'s eyes of understanding. Remove all blindness and spiritual deafness from his/her heart. As a priest of God in _____'s life, I plead Your mercy over his/her sins of failure and rebellion. I claim all of his/her life united together in obedient love and service to the Lord Jesus Christ. May the Spirit of the living God focus His mighty work upon _____ to grant him/her repentance and to set him/her completely free from all that binds him/her.

In the name of the Lord Jesus Christ, I thank you for your answer. Grant me the grace to be persistent and faithful in my intercessions for _____, that You may be glorified through this deliverance. *Amen.*

— *Dr. Mark I. Bubeck*

THE "RULES OF THE VICTOR" PRAYER

In the name of Jesus Christ I claim the "Rule of the Victor" over all spirits and spiritual assignments to interfere, confuse, torment or harm _____. All such assigned spirits must leave now. All vows, spells and curses are cancelled and those who sent them are hereby cut-off from receiving power from darkness in the future. All communications and plans of darkness on earth or the heavenlies are hereby blocked, confused and all curses, spells and assignments will return to the sender. Father God, as Your Word says, I pray a blessing on the sender that they may repent from their evil ways and come to know Your Son Jesus as their Lord and Savior. *Amen.*

— *Unknown*

PRAYER FOR SALVATION OF A FRIEND

Loving Heavenly Father, in the name of our Lord and Savior Jesus Christ I bring _____ before You. I thank You Heavenly Father, that You have sovereign control over _____. I thank You for the qualities of _____ that You have placed in this man/woman.

In the name of the Lord Jesus Christ and as a priest of God, I plead the sufficiency of the blood of Christ to meet the full penalty his/her sins deserve. I claim back the ground of his/her life that he has given to Satan by believing the enemy's deception. In the name of the Lord Jesus

Christ I resist all of Satan's activity to hold _____ in blindness and darkness.

Exercising my authority through my union with the Lord Jesus Christ, I pull down the strongholds which the kingdom of darkness has formed against _____. I smash all those plans formed against _____'s mind, will, emotions, and his/her body. I invite the Holy Spirit of God to bring the fullness of His power to convict, to bring to repentance, and to lead _____ into faith in the Lord Jesus Christ as his/her Savior. I ask you, Heavenly Father, to draw _____ to Yourself.

Believing that Your Holy Spirit is leading me, I claim _____ for You in the name of the Lord Jesus Christ. In Jesus' great name I joyfully lay this prayer before You. *Amen.*

— *Dr. Mark I. Bubeck*

Prayer for Salvation of a Friend II

My dear Heavenly Father, I thank you that you know our hearts and are intimately aware of our needs. I praise you Lord and I seek your favor. You have said that we can come confidently before your throne and, on this day, I bring _____ before you. O Lord, my heart breaks that he/she does not know you. Please hear my prayer and grant this petition.

Jesus, in your word you said that "No one can come to me unless the Father who sent me draws him" *(John 6:44)* and so I ask you to draw _____ unto yourself. I pray Lord, that he/she may seek to know you and that he/she would believe your Word. I ask you to bind Satan so that he may not blind _____ to the truth. Lord, I pray that you bring someone into his/her life who, through Your Holy Spirit, can lead him/her to Christ. I pray, Lord, that he/she will believe in Jesus

Christ as his/her savior. John 5:24 says "I tell you the truth, whoever hears my Word and believes Him who sent me has eternal life and will not be condemned; he has crossed over from death to life."

Heavenly Father, I pray that _____ turns from sin and confesses that Christ is Lord. I pray that he/she will surrender all and follow Christ without reservation. It is my prayer that as _____ studies the Word, that his/her faith will take root and he/she will grow in Christ. These things I pray in your precious name. *Amen.*

— *Kathryn McBride*

PRAYER FOR CHRISTIAN UNITY

Dear God and Father of our Lord Jesus Christ, I worship You in the wonder of Your Triune Oneness. Thank You, blessed Holy Spirit, for Your great work of baptizing me into this body of Christ the church. Thank You, Lord Jesus Christ for continuing Your mighty work of readying Your church, to present her to Yourself as a radiant bride, without stain of any kind.

My Father, I rejoice that Your salvation has united me inseparably not only with Yourself but also with every other believer. Yet I long and pray for the bringing together of Your born-again ones. We have been terribly wounded by those things that have divided us. Thank you, Lord Jesus Christ, for planning for unity rather than uniformity. The diversity of Your body is part of its beauty and appeal to the lost. It adds to Your glory. Help us to love one another in our diversity.

Blessed Heavenly Father, I recognize that Satan and his kingdom are relentless in their efforts to keep believers divisive toward one another. As the accuser of the believers, he continually plants suspicions in believers' hearts. In the name of my Lord Jesus Christ, I pull down that work of darkness and bind our enemy that he might not succeed.

I ask the Holy Spirit to supplant all divisive works active in believers. In Jesus' precious name I pray. *Amen.*

— *Dr. Mark I. Bubeck*

PRAYERS FOR CHILDREN AS THEY SLEEP AT NIGHT

In the name of the Lord Jesus Christ, I commit _____'s mind, will, emotions, and body into the protecting power of the Lord Jesus Christ and the sealing ministry of the Holy Spirit while he/she sleeps. I bind and forbid any powers of darkness from tampering with any part of _____'s person on the conscious, subconscious, and unconscious level. Heavenly Father, assign your holy angels to protect _____'s person and room to insure that no powers of darkness may intrude in any way while he/she sleeps. *Amen.*

— *Dr. Mark I. Bubeck*

PROTECTION FOR CHILDREN FROM VIOLENCE

Heavenly Father, we live in a very wicked world. One of the worst expressions of this evil is the brutal harm done to little children by sinful people. Often it ends in kidnapping, sexual abuse, or even the violent death of the child. Thank You for Your hatred of this despicable evil and for Your holy wrath. I ask You to stand with me in watchful protection against any such evils happening to _____. I have made You my dwelling, and I depend upon You to assign Your holy angels in constant protective care of _____. May the most clever ploy of Satan, and the wicked people he controls, be unable to touch _____ in any way. In the name of our Lord Jesus Christ. *Amen.*

— *Dr. Mark I. Bubeck*

PRAYERS FOR CHILDREN IN UNWHOLESOME RELATIONSHIPS

You have told us in Your Word, Heavenly Father, that "bad company corrupts good character." Because of this truth, I have deep concern for the corrupting influence I see _____ having on _____. In the name of my Lord Jesus Christ, I pull down all relationships between _____ and _____ that are being promoted by the kingdom of darkness. I ask the Lord Jesus Christ to sever all of the unwholesome bonding that is taking place between _____ and _____. I ask that You would sovereignly bring into _____'s life only those wholesome friendships that will help _____'s spiritual development and moral integrity. In the name and worthiness of Jesus I pray. *Amen.*

— *Dr. Mark I. Bubeck*

PRAYERS FOR CHILDREN WITH SEXUAL TENDENCIES

Loving heavenly Father, I thank You for Your high and holy purpose for human sexuality. Through my words, prayers, and conduct grant me the wisdom to convey to my children biblical values concerning their sexuality. In the name of my Lord Jesus Christ and by the power of His blood, I resist all strongholds of sexual pervertedness assigned to manipulate and rule over _____'s sexuality. I specifically resist strongholds of _____. *(Name any sexual tendency observed in your child; i.e., pornography, masturbation, same-sex attraction, etc.)* I command them to cease all activity against _____. They and all their host must leave _____ and go where the Lord Jesus Christ sends them. *Amen.*

— *Dr. Mark I. Bubeck*

Resisting the Enemy on Behalf of a Child

In the name of the Lord Jesus Christ and by the power of His blood, I resist any spirit of darkness that is trying to cause my son or daughter to _____. I forbid you to do it. I command you to leave our presence and go to where Jesus Christ sends you. *Amen.*

— *Unknown*

Prayer for Rebellious Son/Daughter

I bow humbly before the heavenly Father to intercede for my son/ daughter, _____. I bring him/her before You in the name of the Lord Jesus Christ. I thank You that You have loved _____ with the love of Calvary. I thank You that You gave him/her to us to love and nurture in Christ. I ask You to forgive us for all of our failures to guide him/her in the way he/she ought to go. I am thankful that You are sovereign and can use even the depths of sin to which he/she is now enslaved to rebound to your glory. I praise You for this great trial that humbles my heart before You.

Accepting my position of being "mighty through God to the pulling down of strongholds," I bring all of the work of the Lord Jesus Christ to focus directly against the powers of darkness that blind and bind _____. I pray the victory of our Lord's incarnation, crucifixion, resurrection, ascension, and glorification directly against all of Satan's power in _____'s life. I bind up all powers of darkness set to destroying _____, and I loose him/her from their blinding in the name of the Lord Jesus Christ. I invite the blessed Holy Spirit to move upon _____'s heart and to convict him/her of sin, of righteousness, and of judgment to come. In my priestly ministry, I confess _____'s sins unto You and plead Your compassionate mercy toward him/her. I confess his/her yielding to all manner of fleshly sins, which has given Satan such place in his/her life. I plead the blood of Christ over _____'s wickedness and wait upon the Holy Spirit to bring him/her to repentance, faith, and life in the Lord Jesus Christ. By faith, I claim for a life yielded to serve the true and living God in the name of the Lord Jesus Christ. *Amen.*

— *Dr. Mark I. Bubeck*

A FATHER'S PRAYER FOR A DAUGHTER

Loving heavenly Father, I bring my lovely daughter to your throne in prayer. Through the person and work of the Lord Jesus Christ, I present her to You as one made perfect and acceptable unto You. May the blessed Holy Spirit overshadow us during this time of prayer and enable me to pray in the Spirit. I bring all powers of darkness seeking to assault _____ and afflict her to account before the true and living God. I pray for her union with the mighty victory of the Lord Jesus Christ directly against them. All powers of darkness seeking to hurt my daughter's body and soul, I bind up in the name of the Lord Jesus Christ. I loose her from their attack and plead over her the precious blood of the Lord Jesus Christ. As her father and as a priest of God, I claim my place of full authority over all powers of darkness. In Your grace, we receive this experience as one having purpose in the sovereign purpose of God. Teach _____ and our family through this trial. In the name of the Lord Jesus Christ, *Amen.*

— *Unknown*

Protection for Family as They Sleep

O Mighty and Everlasting God, the Father of our Lord Jesus Christ, I thank You that today, by Your divine power, you have preserved me and those that I love from injury and danger. I owe this protection to your mercy alone. I ask you to forgive us of any sins that we have committed against you. Father, in your mercy, protect us from temptation and the schemes of Satan as he seeks to ensnare us. Please defend us against sorrow and anxiety, which Satan would use to bring us into despair. Abba Father, may Your eyes be upon us and may you keep us safe against all violence and assault from the enemy. Lord, protect us. Surround us with Your love. For only in You is our salvation and our help. You, O Lord, are a strong fortress, our sword and shield. All of our hope rests in You. I lift up my eyes and cry out for help from You, the Triune God, who made the heavens and the earth. Be with us this night and surround our home with warrior angels who will keep watch and protect us. Guard our dreams and our thoughts so that they may only be of you. In the precious name of Jesus. *Amen.*

— *Kathryn McBride*

Prayer for Cleansing a Home

In the name of my Lord Jesus Christ, I renounce any claim that any demons may have on this home *(or other property)*. As one with authority over this home and as a child of the King, I renounce the sins that opened a door for any demonic presence in this place. Therefore, in the name of Jesus I command every demon to leave this place now and go where my Lord Jesus Christ sends you. Even now, I invite the Holy Spirit to sweep this place clean and fill it with His presence. I ask that the blessing and peace of God will rest on this place so that it may be a haven of rest, a home blessed by God. In Jesus' name, *Amen.*

— *Dr. Marcus Warner*

PRAYER TO ESTABLISH A SPIRITUAL REFUGE

Almighty and sovereign God and Father of our Lord Jesus Christ. I come before you now in the name of our Savior and in the power of Your Holy Spirit, and ask that You would search out and bring into the light any unconfessed sin or act of wickedness committed in this residence, and that you would drive away by your power any lingering enemy spirits. In Jesus name, I bind any enemies, right now that would seek to exert influence in this dwelling — Father, this is Your property. Cleanse and sanctify this place through the power of the blood of Calvary, and fill it with Your presence and glory. Use this home for your eternal purposes — set guardian angels at the boundaries of this property to shield and protect my family *(name specific family members)* from all evil influence. I proclaim that "the scepter of the wicked" will not remain over this home you have given to us. Through the name that is above every name, King of kings and Lord of lords, Jesus Christ. *Amen.*

— *Unknown*

PROTECTING YOUR HOUSEHOLD

There is a great deal that can be said about protecting your household in the face of spiritual warfare. This is a short list of steps to take to have God's protection:

Confess and renounce any ancestral sins, known or unknown. Cancel Satan's claims on the family because of this. Command all wicked spirits to go to where Christ sends them.

Make sure everyone understands the genuine gospel of Jesus Christ.
• God is creator and Judge.
• God must judge sin.
• Each stands guilty before God if not forgiven in Jesus Christ. SIN
• Christ died to take away our guilt of sin. SUBSTITUTE
• Each one must receive Jesus as Savior. TRUST

If there is a question regarding an individual's salvation, pray for (1) the removal of Satan's blinding, (2) the conviction of the Holy Spirit, and (3) the Father's drawing that individual to trust in Christ.

Set an example of trust and obedience to God's Word and engage in meaningful, relevant prayer with members of the family. Allow members of the family to participate with requests and to express prayer to the Lord.

Treat each member of the household with respect and consideration, patiently treating each according to his/her particular developmental stage and situation.

Pray for God's protective barrier around each member wherever they are and pray that the Holy Spirit will guide them into His way and away from the wrong way. Explain the reality of spiritual warfare, of Christ's power and victory, and how to have victory.

Ask the Lord to cleanse the house from every evil influence. There may have been previous residents who gave access to demons and may have left items there. Seek the Lord's guidance as to what might be a problem. Pray for the removal of any curse or influence and then destroy objects that seem suspicious.

Dedicate the house and the family to the Lord for His control, protection, and blessing. Let praise and joy fill the house. Keep a positive attitude. Play good music such as spiritual songs and classic compositions.

Do not allow the entrance of evil influence into the house and supervise in a gracious but firm method what is played or viewed in the house. Prevent dark, mysterious, and sexually perverse material or influence to enter.

— *Dr. C. Fred Dickason*

PRAYER FOR THE WORKPLACE

Lord Jesus, Great Son of God, in whom I trust for my salvation and eternal life, I thank You for Your love and sovereign grace in my life at this present time; and I trust You for your concerned intervention in the affairs of my life. I trust You for my well-being, my relationships, my family, my responsibilities and my daily needs.

I thank You for the work You have given me to do, for the employment I have. Help me to contribute to the prospering of those for whom I work. Help me to do all that I do as unto You, for You are my Lord and Master who is in charge of my life and my labor. May I continue to work at the place for the benefit of my employers and for my financial benefit as long as it pleases You. I trust You for the course of my life and labor, for I am Your child through Jesus Christ.

Great Shepherd of the sheep, watch over me in this workplace that I may be a testimony to You and Your truth and grace. Let my attitude be that of serving You in all I do. I am concerned about certain evidences and manifestations of evil in this place, and so I bring this request to You. May the forces of evil be routed and their purposes brought to ruin. Destroy the works of the devil in this place. Do not allow that continuation of misuse of authority, lines of communication, and use of funds. Bring conviction by the Holy Spirit to those not in line with your will. Bring to the minds of those in final authority any improper behavior so that correction may take place. Defeat the schemes of Satan and his demons and protect Your people that work here. Let Your angels attend and protect me and my testimony in this place. Give me grace, patience and determination to serve You while I wait for Your intervention. I would appreciate Your acting quickly to alleviate the difficulties that are present here. I submit my requests to You in the name of the Risen and Victorious Savior. I thank You that you hear me and will answer according to Your wise and sovereign counsel. *Amen.*

— *Dr. C. Fred Dickason*

Lack of Purpose and Goals

Thank You, heavenly Father that "All the days ordained for _____ were written in your book before one of them came to be" *(Psalm 139:16)*. I rejoice in Your good and satisfying plan for _____'s future. At the present moment the sense of direction and life purpose for _____ seems hidden from him/her. In the name of the Lord Jesus Christ I resist all efforts of darkness to obscure and misdirect _____'s life into a purposeless future. I ask for You to sovereignly direct and reveal to _____ Your appointed plan for him/her. Grant to _____ the wisdom to discern that plan and to enter into it in obedience to Your will. *Amen.*

— *Dr. Mark I. Bubeck*

Prayer for Marriage

Loving Heavenly Father, I thank You for Your perfect plan for our marriage. I know that a marriage functioning in Your will is fulfilling and beautiful. I bring our marriage before You that You might make it all You desire it to be.

Please forgive me for my sins of failure in our marriage. *(One may specify and enlarge confessions.)* In the name of the Lord Jesus Christ. I tear down all of Satan's strongholds designed to destroy our marriage. In his name, I break all negative relationships between us that have been established by Satan and his wicked spirits. I will accept only the relationship established by You and the blessed Holy Spirit. I invite the Holy Spirit to enable me to relate to _____ *(your spouse's name)* in a manner that will meet his/her needs.

I submit our conversations to You, that they may please You. I submit our physical relationship to You, that it may enjoy Your blessing. I submit our love to You, that You may cause it to grow and mature.

Open my eyes to see all areas where I am deceived. Open _____'s eyes to see any of Satan's deceptions upon him/her. Make our union to be the Christ-centered relationship You have designed in Your perfect will. I ask this in Jesus' name with thanksgiving. *Amen.*

— *Dr. Mark I. Bubeck*

Prayers for Revival

Heavenly Father, I come before You to plead Your mercy over my sins, the sins of other believers, and the sins of our nation. May You judge not this nation with wrath and fury as upon Sodom, but judge it with a mighty outpouring of conviction of sin. May sinners groan under the burden of their guilt until the people cry out as did those at Pentecost, "What shall we do?" I praise Your holy name that there is sufficient measure of grace through the Person and work of the Lord Jesus Christ to answer this cry. I wait for the Holy Spirit to prepare and bring us all to revival. I ask this all with praise in the merit of the Lord Jesus Christ. *Amen.*

* * * * *

Loving Heavenly Father, I see about me brokenness and need. I see great needs in my own heart, in my family, among my fellow believers, and in my community and culture. Teach me to care, and to pray about those needs as Your servant Nehemiah learned to pray. Unveil Your presence among us. Draw near to us that we might experience the brokenness and the awareness of our sinful need. I affirm that revival comes as people become aware of the near presence of our holy God. It's in the name and finished work of our Lord Jesus Christ that I pray. *Amen.*

— *Dr. Mark I. Bubeck*

Prayer for the Country and World

Loving Heavenly Father, I come in humble obedience to use the weapons of my warfare against the darkness that is seeking to rule the people of my city, country, and world. I affirm that the weapons You have given me have divine power that is sufficient to demolish every stronghold Satan has built to hold back Your plan.

In the Lord Jesus Christ's mighty name I use the weapons of my warfare to weaken and demolish every dominion, authority, power of darkness, and wicked spirit in the heavenly realm who has strategized to hinder revival.

In the name of the Lord Jesus Christ and by the power of His blood, I pull down all levels of the stronghold of _____. *(for example: abortion practices and promotion, occult promotion and activity, religious cults and "isms," divorce and family disunity, violence and abuse, pride and spiritual indifference, etc.)*

Heavenly Father, assign holy angels to engage in direct combat against these strongholds of evil. Thank You that, no matter how formidable and threatening the forces of darkness become, those who are with us are always "more" than those who are with them. *Amen.*

— *Dr. Mark I. Bubeck*

Drugs and Other Intoxicants

In the name of my Lord Jesus Christ, I come against those manipulating powers of darkness seeking to create and intensify _____'s dependence upon _____ *(name intoxicant)* to cope with life. I renounce and reject that deception of darkness in _____'s life that has made him/her dependent upon this counterfeit pleasure. I ask the Lord Jesus Christ to evict all powers of darkness associated with _____'s bondage and to send them to the place where they can never control or manipulate him/her again. May the mighty work of the Holy Spirit remove this counterfeit dependence and replace it with the joyful fruit of His full control. *Amen.*

— *Dr. Mark I. Bubeck*

PRAYER FOR BINDING THE ENEMY
During a Renunciation

In the name of my Lord Jesus Christ I bind any demon from in anyway interfering with what Christ wants to do here today. I bind you to inactivity and to silence. You will not harm me or anyone in this room. You will not act out, but will submit to whatever commands you are given as one who has been defeated by the blood of the Lord Jesus Christ.

— *Dr. Marcus Warner*

THE WORD OF GOD

Loving heavenly Father, I come to worship you in the wonder of what You have chosen to reveal in Your Word about Yourself. The majesty of Your creation displays Your awesome greatness. I see Your omnipotence when I look upon the vastness of the Universe. I praise You that You are everywhere present in the extremities of the universe and that You are greater than Your creation.

I look upon the immensity of man's accumulated knowledge and remember Your omniscient possession of all knowledge. The steady march of time causes me to reflect upon the fact that You are eternal, without beginning or end. The lying, sinful ways of humanity evident everywhere causes me to long for the One who is truth and who reigns in absolute justice.

I praise You, loving God and Father of our Lord Jesus Christ, for what You have revealed about Yourself in the written Word of God. I affirm that Your Holy Word is an inerrant revelation of Your holy truth. I ask forgiveness for my neglect in reading, memorizing, and meditating upon Your Word. What an ugly, sinful wrong it is for me, my family, and my fellow believers to treat Your Holy Word so lightly when it has been made so available to us. Wash away our guilt, and create within believers' hearts a longing to know and read Your Word.

Through Your Word heavenly Father, I came to know the Lord Jesus Christ as my Savior from sin. In Your Word, He is revealed as the one who became God in human flesh and was victorious in Himself over the world, the flesh, and the Devil. In Your Word I learn that, though He was emptied in every way I am tempted, He never sinned. Your Word declares that, as one of us, He fulfilled all righteousness. Your Word declares that He was wounded for my transgressions and bruised for my iniquities. It declares that He became sin for me and that my sins and offenses against You were laid upon Him when He died in my place upon the cross.

It is in Your Word that the mighty truth of His triumph over death and the grave in resurrection power is established. Your Word declares with assuring detail the Lord Jesus Christ's ascension into heaven and His present, glorified overseeing of His church. Because of the declarations of Your Word, I look for my Savior to come again with power and great glory. I love You, heavenly Father, for having given me Your Word.

I praise You, loving God, that You have graced us with the coming of the Holy Spirit at Pentecost. Thank You for revealing Your Word to me in the wonder of His mighty work in this world and in believers. Thank You for declaring in Your Word that the Holy Spirit came to convict the word of its sinful guilt. I ask for the Holy Spirit to greatly intensify His work of convincing people of their sin against a holy God. May the Holy Spirit so open people to the spiritual seeing and hearing of Your

Word that they again will cry out in repentance. Thank You, also, that the Holy Spirit exalts righteousness by revealing the righteous things of Your Word. I ask Him to do that with powerful persuasion.

I pray that the Holy Spirit will, by Your Word, reveal to human hearts the certainty of an approaching accountability to God. May that sobering fact settle upon people until they can find no rest apart from coming to our Lord Jesus Christ.

Blessed Holy Spirit, You are the one who breathed out God's Word in divine revelation through human instruments. I ask You now to use that Word to speak personally to believers. Grant new insights to God's appointed leaders to promote interest, reading, memorization and meditation upon God's Word among God's people. I ask You, Holy spirit, to raise up anointed revivalists, evangelists, and preachers who will be able to make the Bible known with compelling power to a lost world.

I pray the mighty power of God's Holy Word against Satan and his Kingdom. Confront and defeat Satan's lies with the truth of Your Word. May the comfort of Your Word relieve people from Satan's accusations, torments, and terror. I ask that the warnings of Your Word will alert people to Satan's tactics to bring them into bondage. Invade Satan's kingdom with salvation's message in Your Word and bring multitudes from the darkness of hell into the kingdom of light and eternal life.

I recognize, heavenly Father, that revival will never come unless a deep, personalized hearing of God's Word comes to human hearts. In the name of my Lord Jesus Christ and by the power of His blood. I pull down Satan's power to dishonor and discredit God's Holy Word. I bring in prayer the power of the Holy Spirit against all satanic strongholds assigned to hinder the Word of God from being heard and understood by the hearts of people. I invite the blessed Holy Spirit to exalt the Word of God and to reveal its mighty power in ways that will confound the enemies of truth. Cause people to hear Your Word with a new, profound depth, and move pastors and churches to proclaim and teach Your Word with a contagious freshness.

I affirm, heavenly Father, that Your Word is alive and powerful. I rejoice that, though heaven and earth will pass away, not one tiny word of Your holy truth will ever fail. Grant to Your Word great success in our day. Use Your Holy Word to move our nation to revolutionary revival. I love Your Word, O Lord, and I give myself to know it better and to live it more. I offer this prayer in the name of Him who is the Living Word, my Lord Jesus Christ. *Amen.*

— *Dr. Mark I. Bubeck*

Chapter Eight

HELP WITH PRAYER

"The church is not a hospital; it's a military outpost under orders to storm the gates of hell. Every believer is on active duty, called to take part in fulfilling the Great Commission (Matthew 28:19, 20). Thankfully the church has an infirmary where we can minister to the weak and wounded, and that ministry is necessary. But our real purpose is to be change agents in the world, taking a stand, living by faith, and accomplishing something for God."

— Dr. Neil T. Anderson

How to Pray in a Crisis Situation

In crisis situations where you suspect demonic bondage in your own life or the life of one close to you, the following procedures have brought release and freedom.

1. Set aside one day a week for fasting and prayer. Enlist others who may share your spiritual burden and concern.

2. Pray a brief doctrinal prayer of this kind each hour on the hour.

"In the name of my Lord Jesus Christ and by the power of His blood, I pull down all deceptive powers of darkness seeking to deceive and control _____ by _____. I command these powers of darkness to cease their wicked work and they must leave _____ and go where my Lord Jesus Christ sends them."

Use whenever you sense barriers or stressed relationships with another: In the name of the Lord Jesus Christ and by the power of His blood, I pull down all barriers and relationships between _____ and me that are being authorized by Satan and the powers of darkness. I will only accept relationships between _____ and me that are authorized by the Holy Spirit in the will of God. *Amen.*

— *Dr. Mark I. Bubeck*

Dr. Karl Payne's "Ground Rule Box"

The Ground Rule Box is the list of ground rules that Dr. Payne uses to bring demons under complete submission to the authority of Christ in a deliverance session.

• In the name of the Lord Jesus Christ we bind the strongman. He will not be allowed to interfere in this process in any way. There will be no

outside reinforcements of any kind. If there are demons involved with
_____ you are on trial and you are going to lose.

- In the name of the Lord Jesus Christ, there will be one-way traffic only, from _____ to the pit. When you leave you will take all of your works and effects and all of your associates and their works and effects with you. You will not be free to re-enter _____ or to enter anyone else in the room.

- In the name of the Lord Jesus Christ you may speak only that which may be used against you.

- In the name of the Lord Jesus Christ, the answers you give must stand as truth before the white throne of God.

- In the name of the Lord Jesus Christ, there will be no profanity.

- In the name of the Lord Jesus Christ, _____ is to have complete and full control of his/her tongue, mind and body. You will not be allowed to control his tongue, mind or body.

- In the name of the Lord Jesus Christ, I will give commands stating "We command" because this is _____'s fight. The Holy Spirit of God is going before us, and we stand as a majority, and we stand together against you. _____ does not want anything to do with you. _____ is a child of God who stands against you. You are an unwanted intruder who is going to have to leave upon command.

- In the name of the Lord Jesus Christ, when I give commands you will give clear, concise, complete answers in _____'s mind to the questions addressed to you. You will not be permitted to confuse the mind of _____ and will be punished severely by the Holy Spirit of God if you attempt to do so

- When I give commands in the name of the Lord Jesus Christ you will clearly give your answers to _____. You do not have the privilege of speaking directly through him in this confrontation.

- In the name of the Lord Jesus Christ, there will be no hiding, duplicating, or changing of authority and rank. We bind you by the authority structure you now have, and that structure will only be altered if we choose to change it.

- In the name of the Lord Jesus Christ, when I give commands for you to answer, you will give your answers to _____ who will share your responses with me. I will not speak directly to you; you are a defeated enemy not a colleague or an equal, and you are not worth speaking to. I will speak to my brother/sister in Christ. The only thing you are going to do is cooperate under the ground rules. Your authority is smashed!

- Lastly. In the name of the Lord Jesus Christ, we ask the Holy Spirit of God to enforce all of the ground rules and to punish severely any demons who attempt to step outside of the ground rule box.

Four Declarations (to accompany the Ground Rules)

- We declare our victory over all the powers of darkness through our head, the Lord Jesus Christ. We declare that the Lord Jesus Christ has smashed the authority of Satan at the cross of Calvary where He made an open spectacle of your master. Colossians 2:13-15 states: *And when you were dead in your transgressions and the uncircumcision of your flesh, He made you alive together with Him, having forgiven us all of our transgressions, having cancelled out the certificate of debt consisting of decrees against us and which was hostile to us; and He has taken it out of the way, having nailed it to the cross. When He had disarmed the rulers and authorities, He made a public spectacle of them, having triumphed over them through Him.*

- We declare our authority over the powers of darkness through our Lord Jesus Christ. In Luke 10:18-20 Jesus told those who follow Him: *And He said to them, I was watching Satan fall from heaven like lightning. Behold, I have given you authority to tread upon serpents and scorpions, and over all the power of the enemy, and nothing shall injure you. Nevertheless do not rejoice in this, that the spirits are subject to you, but rejoice that your names are recorded in heaven.*

- From the same Luke 10 passage we declare our protection from the powers of darkness through our head, the Lord Jesus Christ. Jesus said, "and nothing shall injure you." We declare this to be true through our Lord Jesus Christ and stand upon it.

- We declare our position over the powers of darkness in Jesus Christ. Jesus Christ is our head and we make up His body. Ephesians 1:18-23 says: *I pray that the eyes of your heart may be enlightened, so that you may know what is the hope of His calling, what are the riches of the glory of His inheritance in the saints, and what is the surpassing greatness of His power toward us who believe. These are in accordance with the working of the strength of His might which He brought about in Christ, when He raised Him from the dead, and seated Him at His right hand in the heavenly places, far above all rule and authority and power and dominion, and every name that is named, not only in this age, but also in the one to come. And He put all things in subjection under His feet, and gave Him as head over all things to the church which is His body, the fullness of Him who fills all in all.*

— *Taken from "Spiritual Warfare: Christians, Demonization and Deliverance" by Dr. Karl Payne*

HOW TO PRAY
by R.A. Torrey

In the 6th chapter of Ephesians in the 18th verse we read words which put the tremendous importance of prayer with startling and over-whelming force: "Praying always with all prayer and supplication in the Spirit, and watching thereunto with all perseverance and supplication for all saints." When we stop to weigh the meaning of these words, then note the connection in which they are found, the intelligent child of God is driven to say, "I must pray, pray, pray. I must put all my energy and all my heart into prayer. Whatever else I do, I must pray." The Revised Version is, if possible, stronger than the Authorized: "With all prayer and supplication praying at all seasons in the spirit, and watching thereunto in all perseverance and supplication for all the saints."

Note the ALLS: "with ALL prayer," "at ALL seasons," "in ALL perseverance," "for ALL the saints." Note the piling up of strong words, "prayer," "supplication," "perseverance." Note once more the strong expression, "watching thereunto," more literally, "being sleepless thereunto." Paul realized the natural slothfulness of man, and especially his natural slothfulness in prayer. How seldom we pray things through! How often the church and the individual get right up to the verge of a great blessing in prayer and just then let go, get drowsy, quit. I wish that these words "being sleepless unto prayer" might burn into our hearts. I wish the whole verse might burn into our hearts.

But why is this constant, persistent, sleepless, overcoming prayer so needful?

1. First of all, because there is a devil. He is cunning, he is mighty, he never rests, he is ever plotting the downfall of the child of God; and if the child of God relaxes in prayer, the devil will succeed in ensnaring him.

This is the thought of the context. The 12th verse reads: "For our wrestling is not against flesh and blood, but against the principalities, against the powers, against the world rulers of this darkness, against the spiritual hosts of wickedness in the heavenly places." Then comes the 13th verse: "Wherefore take up the whole armor of God, that ye may be able to withstand in the evil day, and, having done all, to stand." Next follows a description of the different parts of the Christian's armor, which we are to put on if we are to stand against the devil and his mighty wiles. Then Paul brings all to a climax in the

18th verse, telling us that to all else we must add prayer—constant, persistent, untiring, sleepless prayer in the Holy Spirit, or all else will go for nothing.

2. Prayer is God's appointed way for obtaining things, and the great secret of all lack in our experience, in our life and in our work is neglect of prayer.

James brings this out very forcibly in the 4th chapter and 2nd verse of his epistle: "Ye have not because ye ask not." These words contain the secret of the poverty and powerlessness of the average Christian—neglect of prayer. "Why is it," many a Christian is asking, "I make so little progress in my Christian life?" "Neglect of prayer," God answers. "You have not because you ask not." "Why is it," many a minister is asking, "I see so little fruit from my labors?" Again God answers, "Neglect of prayer. You have not because you ask not."

3. Those men whom God set forth as a pattern of what he expected Christians to be—the apostles—regarded prayer as the most important business of their lives.

All the mighty men of God of the Bible have been men of prayer. They have differed from one another in many things, but in this they have been alike.

4. Prayer occupied a very prominent place and played a very important part in the earthly life of our Lord.

The words "pray" and "prayer" are used at least twenty-five times in connection with our Lord in the brief record of His life in the four Gospels, and His praying is mentioned in places where the words are not used. Evidently prayer took much of the time and strength of Jesus, and a man or woman who does not spend much time in prayer, cannot properly be called a follower of Jesus Christ.

5. Praying is the most important part of the present ministry of our risen Lord.

Christ's ministry did not close with His death. His atoning work was finished then, but when He rose and ascended to the right hand of the Father, He entered upon other work for us just as important in its place as His atoning work. It cannot be divorced from His atoning work; it rests upon that as its basis, but it is necessary to our complete salvation. The same thought is found in Paul's remarkable, triumphant challenge in Romans 8:34 —"Who is he that shall condemn? It is Christ Jesus that died, yea rather, that was raised from the dead, who is at the right hand of God, Who also maketh intercession for us."

If we then are to have fellowship with Jesus Christ in His present work, we must spend much time in prayer; we must give ourselves to earnest, constant, persistent, sleepless, overcoming prayer. I know of nothing that has so impressed me with a sense of the importance of praying at all seasons, being much and constantly in prayer, as the thought that that is the principal occupation at present of my risen Lord. I want to have fellowship with Him, and to that end I have asked the Father that whatever else He may make me, to make me at all events an intercessor, to make me a man who knows how to pray, and who spends much time in prayer.

6. Prayer is the means that God has appointed for our receiving mercy, and obtaining grace to help in time of need.

Hebrews 4:16 is one of the simplest and sweetest verses in the Bible, — "Let us therefore come boldly unto the throne of grace, that we may obtain mercy, and find grace to help in time of need." These words make it very plain that God has appointed a way by which we shall seek and obtain mercy and grace. That way is prayer; bold, confident, outspoken approach to the throne of grace, the most holy place of God's presence, where our sympathizing High Priest, Jesus Christ, has entered in our behalf. *(Verses 14, 15.)* Mercy is what we need, grace is what we must have, or all our life and effort will end in complete failure. Prayer is the way to get them. There is infinite grace at our disposal, and we make it ours experimentally by prayer. Oh, if we only realized the fullness of God's grace, that is ours for the asking, its height and depth and length and breadth, I am sure that we would spend more time in prayer. The measure of our appropriation of grace is determined by the measure of our prayers. Who is there that does not feel that he needs more grace? Then ask for it. Be constant and persistent in your asking. Be importunate and untiring in your asking. God delights to have us "shameless" beggars in this direction; for it shows our faith in Him, and He is mightily pleased with faith. Because of our "shamelessness" He will rise and give us as much as we need *(Luke 11:8)*. What little streams of mercy and grace most of us know, when we might know rivers overflowing their banks!

7. Prayer in the name of Jesus Christ is the way Jesus Christ himself has appointed for his disciples to obtain fullness of joy.

He states this simply and beautifully in John 16:24, "Hitherto have ye asked nothing in My name; ask, and ye shall receive, that your joy may be fulfilled." "Made full" is the way the Revised Version reads. Who is there that does not wish his joy filled full? Well, the way to have it filled full is by praying in the name of Jesus. There is no greater joy on earth or in heaven, than communion with God, and prayer in the name of Jesus brings us into communion with Him.

8. Prayer, in every care and anxiety and need of life, with thanksgiving, is the means that God has appointed for obtaining freedom from all anxiety, and the peace of God which passeth all understanding.

"Be careful for nothing," says Paul, "but in everything by prayer and supplication with thanksgiving let your requests be made known unto God, and the peace of God which passeth all understanding, shall keep your hearts and minds through Christ Jesus." *(Philippians 4:6-7.)* To many this seems at the first glance, the picture of a life that is beautiful, but beyond the reach of ordinary mortals; not so at all. The verse tells us how the life is attainable by every child of God: "Be careful for nothing," or as the Revised Version reads, "In nothing be anxious." The remainder of the verse tells us how, and it is very simple: "But in everything by prayer and supplication with thanksgiving let your requests be made known unto God." What could be plainer or more simple than that? Just keep in constant touch with God, and when any trouble or vexation, great or small, comes up, speak to Him about it, never forgetting to return thanks for what He has already done. What will the result be? "The peace of God which passeth all understanding shall guard your hearts and your thoughts in Christ Jesus."

9. Because of what prayer accomplishes.

(1) PRAYER PROMOTES OUR SPIRITUAL GROWTH as almost nothing else, indeed as nothing else but Bible study; and true prayer and true Bible study go hand in hand. John Welch, son-in-law to John Knox, was one of the most faithful men of prayer this world ever saw. He counted that day ill-spent in which seven or eight hours were not used alone with God in prayer and the study of His Word. An old man speaking of him after his death said, "He was a type of Christ." How came he to be so like his Master? His prayer life explains the mystery.

(2) PRAYER BRINGS POWER INTO OUR WORK. If we wish power for any work to which God calls us, be it preaching, teaching, personal work, or the rearing of our children, we can get it by earnest prayer.

(3) PRAYER AVAILS FOR THE CONVERSION OF OTHERS. Prayer often avails where everything else fails. How utterly all of Monica's efforts and entreaties failed with her son, but her prayers prevailed with God, and the dissolute youth became St. Augustine, the mighty man of God. By prayer the bitterest enemies of the Gospel have become its most valiant defenders, the greatest scoundrels the truest sons of God, and the vilest women the purest saints. Oh, the power of prayer to reach down, down, down, where hope itself seems vain, and lift men and women up, up, up into fellowship with and likeness to God. It is simply wonderful! How little we appreciate this marvelous weapon!

(4) PRAYER BRINGS BLESSINGS TO THE CHURCH. The history of the church has always been a history of grave difficulties to overcome. The devil hates the church and seeks in every way to block its progress; now by false doctrine, again by division, again by inward corruption of life. But by prayer, a clear way can be made through everything. Prayer will root out heresy, allay misunderstanding, sweep away jealousies and animosities, obliterate immoralities, and bring in the full tide of God's reviving grace. History abundantly proves this. In the hour of darkest portent, when the case of the church, local or universal, has seemed beyond hope, believing men and believing women have met together and cried to God and the answer has come.

It was so in the days of Knox, it was so in the days of Wesley and Whitfield, it was so in the days of Edwards and Brainerd, it was so in the days of Finney, it was so in the days of the great revival of 1857 in this country and of 1859 in Ireland, and it will be so again in your day and mine. Satan has marshalled his forces. The world, the flesh and the devil are holding high carnival. It is now a dark day, BUT—now "it is time for Thee, Lord, to work; for they have made void Thy law." *(Psalm 119:126)*. And He is getting ready to work, and now He is listening for the voice of prayer. Will He hear it? Will He hear it from you? Will He hear it from the church as a body? I believe He will.

— *Taken from "How to Pray" by R. A. Torrey*

WHY ME?

Why should I say I can't when the Bible says I can do all things through Christ who gives me strength?
—*Philippians 4:13*

Why should I worry about my needs when I know that God will take care of all of my needs according to His riches in glory in Christ Jesus?
—*Philippians 4:19*

Why should I fear when the Bible says God has not given me a spirit of fear, but of power, love and a sound mind?
—*2 Timothy 1:7*

Why should I lack faith to allow Christ to live His life through me, when God has given me a measure of faith?
—*Romans 12:3*

Why should I be weak when the Bible says that the Lord is the strength of my life and that I will display strength and take action because I know God?
—*Psalm 28:7*

Why should I allow Satan control over my life when He that is in me is greater than he that is in the world?
—*1 John 4:4*

Why should I accept defeat when the Bible says that God always leads me in victory?
—*2 Corinthians 2:14*

Why should I lack wisdom when I know that Christ became wisdom to me from God and God gives wisdom to me generously when I ask Him for it?
—*1 Corinthians 1:30; James 1:5*

Why should I be depressed when I can recall to mind God's loving-kindness, compassion, and faithfulness and have hope?
—*Lamentations 3:21-23*

Why should I worry and be upset when I cast all my anxiety on Christ who cares for me?
—*1 Peter: 5:7*

Why should I ever be in bondage knowing that there is liberty and freedom where the Spirit of the Lord is?
—*2 Corinthians 3:17; Galatians 5:1*

Why should I feel condemned when the Bible says there is no
condemnation for those who are in Christ Jesus?
—*Romans 8:1*

Why should I feel alone when Jesus said He is with me always and
He will never leave me nor forsake me?
—*Matthew 28:20; Hebrew 13:5*

Why should I feel like I am cursed or the victim of misfortune when
the Bible says that Christ rescued me from the curse of the law that
I might receive His Spirit by faith?
—*Galatians 3:13-14*

Why should I be unhappy when I like Paul can learn to be content
whatever the circumstances?
—*Philippians 4:11*

Why should I feel worthless when Christ became sin for me so that
I might become the righteousness of God in Him?
—*2 Corinthians 5:21*

Why should I feel helpless in the presence of others, when I know that
if God is for me, who can be against me?
—*Romans 8:31*

Why should I be confused when God is the author of peace and
He gives me knowledge through His Spirit who lives in me?
—*1 Corinthians 2:12; 14:33*

Why should I feel like a failure when I am more than a conqueror
through Christ who loves me?
—*Romans 8:37*

Why should I let the pressures of life bother me when I can take
courage knowing that Jesus has overcome the world and its problems?
—*John 16:33*

The Promises of God

It's Impossible:	All things are possible. —*Luke 18:27*
I'm Too Tired:	I will give you rest.—*Matthew 11:28-30*
Nobody Really Loves Me:	I Love you. —*John 3:16*
I Can't Go On:	My grace is sufficient.—*2 Corinthians 12:9*
I Can't Figure Things Out:	I will direct your steps. —*Proverbs 3,5, 6*
I Can't Do It:	You can do all things. —*Philippians 4:13*
I'm Not Able:	I am able. —*2 Corinthians 9:8*
It's Not Worth It	It will be worth it. —*Romans 8:28*
I Can't Forgive Myself:	I forgive you. —*1 John 1:9; Romans 8:1*
I Can't Manage:	I will supply all your needs. —*Philippians 4:19*
I'm Afraid:	I have not given you a spirit of fear. —*2 Timothy 1:7*
I'm Always Worried and Frustrated:	Cast all your cares on me. —*1 Peter 5:7*
I Don't Have Enough Faith:	I have given everyone a measure of faith. — *Romans 10:17*
I'm Not Smart Enough:	I give you wisdom. —*1 Corinthians 1:30*
I Feel All Alone:	I will never leave you or forsake you. —*Hebrews 13:5*

— Unknown

WHO I AM IN CHRIST

I Am Accepted:

John 1:12	I am God's child.
John 15:15	I am Christ's friend.
Romans 5:1	I have been justified.
1 Corinthians 6:17	I am united with the Lord, and I am one spirit with Him.
1 Corinthians 6:20	I have been bought with a price. I belong to God.
1 Corinthians 12:27	I am a member of Christ's body.
Ephesians 1:1	I am a saint.
Ephesians 1:5	I have been adopted as God's child.
Ephesians 2:18	I have direct access to God through the Holy Spirit.
Colossians 1:14	I have been redeemed and forgiven of all my sins.
Colossians 2:10	I am complete in Christ.

I Am Secure:

Romans 8:1-2	I am free forever from condemnation.
Romans 8:28	I am assured that all things work together for good.
Romans 8:31-34	I am free from any condemning charges against me.
Romans 8:35-39	I cannot be separated from the love of God.
2 Corinthians 1:21-22	I have been established, anointed, and sealed by God.
Philippians 1:6	I am confident that the good work that God has begun in me will be perfected.
Philippians 3:20	I am a citizen of heaven.

Colossians 3:3	I am hidden with Christ in God.
2 Timothy 1:7	I have not been given a spirit of fear, but of power, love and a sound mind.
Hebrews 4:16	I can find grace and mercy in time of need.
1 John 5:18	I am born of God, and the evil one cannot touch me.

I Am Significant:

Matthew 5:13-14	I am the salt and light of the earth.
John 15:1, 5	I am a branch of the true vine, a channel of His life.
John 15:16	I have been chosen and appointed to bear fruit.
Acts 1:8	I am a personal witness of Christ.
1 Corinthians 3:16	I am God's temple.
2 Corinthians 5:17-21	I am a minster of reconciliation for God.
2 Corinthians 6:1	I am God's co-worker *(1 Corinthians 3:9)*.
Ephesians 2:6	I am seated with Christ in the heavenly realm.
Ephesians 2:10	I am God's workmanship.
Ephesians 3:12	I may approach God with freedom and confidence.
Philippians 4:13	I can do all things through Christ who strengthens me.

— Taken from "Victory Over the Darkness" by Dr. Neil T. Anderson

THE HEART GOD REVIVES

Nancy Leigh DeMoss contrasts characteristics of proud, unbroken people who are resistant to the call of God on their lives with the qualities of broken, humble people who have experienced God's revival. Read each item on the list as you ask God to reveal which characteristics of a proud spirit He finds in your life. Confess these to Him, then ask Him to restore the corresponding quality of a broken humble spirit in you.

"The sacrifices of God are a broken spirit; a broken and a contrite heart, O God, Thou will not despise." Psalm 51:17

Proud People	Broken People
• Focus on the failures of others	• Overwhelmed with a sense of their own spiritual need
• A critical, fault-finding spirit; look at everyone else's faults with a microscope, but their own with a telescope	• Compassionate; can forgive much because they know how much they have been forgiven
• Self-righteous; look down on others	• Esteem all others better than themselves
• Independent, self-sufficient spirit	• Have a dependent spirit; recognize their need for others
• Have to prove that they are right	• Willing to yield the right to be right
• Claim rights; have a demanding spirit	• Yield their rights; have a meek spirit
• Self-protective of their time, their rights and their reputation	• Self-denying
• Desire to be served	• Motivated to serve others
• Desire to be a success	• Motivated to be faithful and to make others a success

Proud People

- Desire self-advancement

- Have drive to be recognized and appreciated

- Wounded when others are promoted and they are overlooked

- Have a subconscious feeling, "This ministry/church is privileged to have me and my gifts;" think of what they can do for God

- Feel confident in how much they know

- Self-conscious

- Keep others at arms' length

- Quick to blame others

- Unapproachable or defensive when criticized

- Concerned with being respectable, with what others think; work to protect their own image and reputation

- Find it difficult to share their spiritual need with others

Broken People

- Desire to promote others

- Have a sense of their own unworthiness; thrilled that God would use them at all

- Eager for others to get the credit; rejoice when others are lifted up

- Heart attitude is, "I don't deserve to have a part in any ministry;" know that they have nothing to offer God except the life of Jesus flowing through their broken lives

- Humbled by how very much they have to learn

- Not concerned with self at all

- Willing to risk getting close to others and to take risks of loving intimately

- Accept personal responsibility and can see where they are wrong in a situation

- Receive criticism with a humble, open spirit

- Concerned with being real; what matters to them is not what others think but what God knows; are willing to die to their own reputation

- Willing to be open and transparent with others as God directs

Proud People

- Want to be sure that no one finds out when they have sinned; their instinct is to cover up

- Have a hard time saying, "I was wrong; will you please forgive me?"

- Tend to deal in generalities when confessing sin

- Concerned about the consequences of their sin

- Remorseful over their sin, sorry that they were found out or caught

- Waits for the other to come and ask forgiveness when there is a misunderstanding or conflict in a relationship

- Compare themselves with others and feel worthy of honor

- Blind to their true heart condition

- Don't think they have anything to repent of

- Don't think they need revival, but are sure that everyone else does

Broken People

- Once broken, don't care who know or who finds out; are willing to be exposed because they have nothing to lose

- Quick to admit failure and to seek forgiveness when necessary

- Able to acknowledge specifics when confessing their sin

- Grieved over the cause, the root of their sin

- Truly, genuinely repentant over their sin, evidenced in the fact that they forsake that sin

- Take the initiative to be reconciled when there is a misunderstanding or conflict in relationships; they race to the cross; they see if they can get there first, no matter how wrong the other may have been

- Compare themselves to the holiness of God and feel a desperate need for His mercy

- Walk in the light

- Realize they have need of a continual heart attitude of repentance

- Continually sense their need for a fresh encounter with God and for a fresh filling of His Holy Spirit

Battle for the Mind

For though we walk in the flesh, we are not waging war according to
the flesh.
—2 Corinthians 10:3

For the weapons of our warfare are not of the flesh but have divine
power to destroy strongholds.
—2 Corinthians 10:4

We destroy arguments and every lofty opinion raised against the
knowledge of God, and take every thought captive to obey Christ.
—2 Corinthians 10:5

Do not be conformed to this world, but be transformed by the renewal
of your mind, that by testing you may discern what is the will of God,
what is good and acceptable and perfect.
—Romans 12:2

For by the grace given to me I say to everyone among you not to
think of himself more highly than he ought to think, but to think
with sober judgment, each according to the measure of faith that
God has assigned.
—Romans 12:3

For those who live according to the flesh set their minds on the things
of the flesh, but those who live according to the Spirit set their minds
on the things of the Spirit.
—Romans 8:5

For to set the mind on the flesh is death, but to set the mind on the
Spirit is life and peace.
—Romans 8:6

For the mind that is set on the flesh is hostile to God, for it does not
submit to God's law; indeed, it cannot.
—Romans 8:7

If then you have been raised with Christ, seek the things that are above, where Christ is, seated at the right hand of God.
—*Colossians 3:1*

Set your minds on things that are above, not on things that are on earth.
—*Colossians 3:2*

But I say, walk by the Spirit, and you will not gratify the desires of the flesh.
—*Galatians 5:16*

to put off your old self, which belongs to your former manner of life and is corrupt through deceitful desires,
—*Ephesians 4:22*

and to be renewed in the spirit of your minds,
—*Ephesians 4:23*

and to put on the new self, created after the likeness of God in true righteousness and holiness.
—*Ephesians 4:24*

Finally, brothers, whatever is true, whatever is honorable, whatever is just, whatever is pure, whatever is lovely, whatever is commendable, if there is any excellence, if there is anything worthy of praise, think about these things.
—*Philippians 4:8*

for God gave us a spirit not of fear but of power and love and self-control.
—*2 Timothy 1:7*

for which I was appointed a preacher and apostle and teacher,
—*2 Timothy 1:11*

which is why I suffer as I do. But I am not ashamed, for I know whom I have believed, and I am convinced that he is able to guard until that day what has been entrusted to me.

—*2 Timothy 1:12*

Therefore, preparing your minds for action, and being sober-minded, set your hope fully on the grace that will be brought to you at the revelation of Jesus Christ.

—*1 Peter 1:13*

The end of all things is at hand; therefore be self-controlled and sober-minded for the sake of your prayers.

—*1 Peter 4:7*

— *Unknown*

Chapter Nine

SCRIPTURE

"If I profess with the loudest voice and clearest exposition every portion of the truth of God except precisely that little point which the world and the devil are at that moment attacking, I am not confessing Christ, however boldly I may be professing Christ. Where the battle rages, there the loyalty of the soldier is proved; and to be steady on all the battlefield besides is mere flight and disgrace if he flinches at that point."

— Martin Luther

I am with you and will watch over you wherever you go, and I will bring you back to this land. I will not leave you until I have done what I have promised you.

— *Genesis 28:15*

But from there you will seek the Lord your God and you will find him, if you search after him with all your heart and with all your soul.

— *Deuteronomy 4:29*

Have I not commanded you? Be strong and courageous. Do not be afraid; do not be discouraged, for the Lord your God will be with you wherever you go.

— *Joshua 1:9*

May I be strong and courageous; may I not be afraid or discouraged because of my adversaries; there is a greater power with me than with them, for You, Lord my God, are with me to help me.

— *2 Chronicles 32:7-8*

I will give thanks to the Lord with my whole heart; I will recount all of your wonderful deeds. I will be glad and exult in you; I will sing praise to your name, O Most High. When my enemies turn back, they stumble and perish before your presence. For you have maintained my just cause; you have sat on the throne, giving righteous judgment. You have rebuked the nations; you have made the wicked perish; you have blotted out their name forever and ever. The enemy came to an end in everlasting ruins; their cities you rooted out; the very memory of them has perished. But the Lord sits enthroned forever; he has established his throne for justice, and he judges the world with righteousness; he judges the peoples with uprightness. The Lord is a stronghold for the oppressed, a stronghold in times of trouble. And those who know your name put their trust in you, for you, O Lord, have not forsaken those who seek you. Sing praises to the Lord, who sits enthroned in Zion! Tell among the peoples his deeds! For he who avenges blood is mindful of them; he does not forget the cry of the afflicted. Be gracious to me, O Lord! See my affliction from those who hate me, O you who lift me up from the gates of death, that I may recount all your praises, that in the gates of the daughter of Zion I may rejoice in your salvation. The nations have sunk in the pit that they made; in the net that they hid, their own foot has been caught. The Lord has made himself known; he has executed judgment; the wicked are snared in the work of their own hands. The wicked shall return to Sheol, all the nations that forget God. For the needy shall not always be forgotten, and the hope of the poor shall not perish forever. Arise, O Lord! Let not man prevail; let the nations be judged before you! Put them in fear, O Lord! Let the nations know that they are but men!

— *Psalm 9*

Love the Lord, all his faithful people! The Lord preserves those who are true to him, but the proud he pays back in full. Be strong and take heart, all you who hope in the Lord.

— *Psalm 31:23-24*

I will bless the Lord at all times; his praise shall continually be in my mouth. My soul makes its boast in the Lord; let the humble hear and be glad. Oh, magnify the Lord with me, and let us exalt his name together! I sought the Lord, and he answered me and delivered me from all my fears. Those who look to him are radiant, and their faces shall never be ashamed. This poor man cried, and the Lord heard him and saved him out of all his troubles. The angel of the Lord encamps around those who fear him, and delivers them. Oh, taste and see that the Lord is good! Blessed is the man who takes refuge in him! Oh, fear the Lord, you his saints, for those who fear him have no lack! The young lions suffer want and hunger; but those who seek the Lord lack no good thing. Come, O children, listen to me; I will teach you the fear of the Lord. What man is there who desires life and loves many days, that he may see good? Keep your tongue from evil and your lips from speaking deceit. Turn away from evil and do good; seek peace and pursue it. The eyes of the Lord are toward the righteous and his ears toward their cry. The face of the Lord is against those who do evil, to cut off the memory of them from the earth. When the righteous cry for help, the Lord hears and delivers them out of all their troubles. The Lord is near to the brokenhearted and saves the crushed in spirit. Many are the afflictions of the righteous, but the Lord delivers him out of them all. He keeps all his bones; not one of them is broken. Affliction will slay the wicked, and those who hate the righteous will be condemned. The Lord redeems the life of his servants; none of those who take refuge in him will be condemned.

— *Psalm 34*

Do not fret because of those who are evil or be envious of those who do wrong; for like the grass they will soon wither, like green plants they will soon die away. Trust in the Lord and do good; dwell in the land and enjoy safe pasture. Take delight in the Lord, and he will give you the desires of your heart. Commit your way to the Lord; trust in him and he will do this: He will make your righteous reward shine like the dawn, your vindication like the noonday sun. Be still before the Lord and wait patiently for him; do not fret when people succeed in their ways, when they carry out their wicked schemes. Refrain from anger and turn from wrath; do not fret—it leads only to evil. For those who are evil will be destroyed, but those who hope in the Lord will inherit the land. A little while, and the wicked will be no more; though you look for them, they will not be found. But the meek will inherit the land and enjoy peace and prosperity. The wicked plot against the righteous and gnash their teeth at them; but the Lord laughs at the wicked, for he knows their day is coming. The wicked draw the sword and bend the bow to bring down the poor and needy, to slay those whose ways are upright. But their swords will pierce their own hearts, and their bows will be broken. Better the little that the righteous have than the wealth of many wicked; for the power of the wicked will be broken, but the Lord upholds the righteous. The blameless spend their days under the Lord's care, and their inheritance will endure forever. In times of disaster they will not wither; in days of famine they will enjoy plenty. But the wicked will perish: Though the Lord's enemies are like the flowers of the field, they will be consumed, they will go up in smoke. The wicked borrow and do not repay, but the righteous give generously; those the Lord blesses will inherit the land, but those he curses will be destroyed. The Lord makes firm the steps of the one who delights in him; though he may stumble, he will not fall, for the Lord upholds him with his hand. I was young and now I am old, yet I have never seen the righteous forsaken or their children begging bread. They are always generous and lend freely; their children will be a blessing. Turn from evil and do good; then you will dwell in the land forever. For the Lord loves the just and will not forsake his faithful ones. Wrongdoers will be completely destroyed, the offspring of the wicked will perish. The righteous will inherit the land and dwell in it forever. The mouths of the righteous utter wisdom, and their tongues speak what is just. The law of their God is in their hearts; their feet do not slip. The wicked lie in wait for the righteous intent on putting them to death; but the Lord will not leave them in the power of the wicked or let them be condemned when brought to trial. Hope in the Lord and keep his way. He will exalt you to inherit the land; when the wicked are destroyed, you will see it. I have seen a wicked and ruthless man flourishing like a luxuriant native tree, but he soon passed away and was no more; though I looked for him, he could not be found. Consider the blameless, observe the upright; a future awaits those who seek peace. But all sinners will be destroyed; there will be no future for the wicked. The salvation of the righteous comes from the Lord; he is their stronghold in time of trouble. The Lord helps them and delivers them; he delivers them from the wicked and saves them, because they take refuge in him.

— *Psalm 37*

I waited patiently for the Lord; he turned to me and heard my cry. He lifted me out of the slimy pit, out of the mud and mire; he set my feet on a rock and gave me a firm place to stand. He put a new song in my mouth, a hymn of praise to our God. Many will see and fear the Lord and put their trust in him. Blessed is the one who trusts in the Lord, who does not look to the proud, to those who turn aside to false gods. Many, Lord my God, are the wonders you have done, the things you planned for us. None can compare with you; were I to speak and tell of your deeds, they would be too many to declare.

— *Psalm 40:1-5*

God is our refuge and strength, an ever-present help in trouble. Therefore we will not fear, though the earth give way and the mountains fall into the heart of the sea, though its waters roar and foam and the mountains quake with their surging. There is a river whose streams make glad the city of God, the holy place where the Most High dwells. God is within her, she will not fall; God will help her at break of day.

— *Psalm 46:1-5*

Be still, and know that I am God; I will be exalted among the nations, I will be exalted in the earth. The Lord Almighty is with us; the God of Jacob is our fortress.

— *Psalm 46:10-11*

Your righteousness, O God, reaches the high heavens. You who have done great things, O God, who is like you?

— *Psalm 71:19*

He who dwells in the shelter of the Most High will abide in the shadow of the Almighty. I will say to the Lord, "My refuge and my fortress, my God, in whom I trust." For he will deliver you from the snare of the fowler and from the deadly pestilence. He will cover you with his pinions, and under his wings you will find refuge; his faithfulness is a shield and buckler. You will not fear the terror of the night, nor the arrow that flies by day, nor the pestilence that stalks in darkness, nor the destruction that wastes at noonday. A thousand may fall at your side, ten thousand at your right hand, but it will not come near you. You will only look with your eyes and see the recompense of the wicked. Because you have made the Lord your dwelling place — the Most High, who is my refuge — no evil shall be allowed to befall you, no plague come near your tent. For he will command his angels concerning you to guard you in all your ways. On their hands they will bear you up, lest you strike your foot against a stone. You will tread on the lion and the adder; the young lion and the serpent you will trample underfoot. "Because he holds fast to me in love, I will deliver him; I will protect him, because he knows my name. When he calls to me, I will answer him; I will be with him in trouble; I will rescue him and honor him. With long life I will satisfy him and show him my salvation."

— *Psalm 91*

Look to the Lord and his strength; seek his face always.
— *Psalm 105:4*

Let me hear Your unfailing love in the morning, For I have put my trust in you. Show me the way that I should walk, for to You I lift up my soul.
— *Psalm 143:8*

I took you from the ends of the earth, from its farthest corners I called you. I said, "You are my servant;" I have chosen you and have not rejected you. So do not fear, for I am with you; do not be dismayed, for I am your God. I will strengthen you and help you; I will uphold you with my righteous right hand. "All who rage against you will surely be ashamed and disgraced; those who oppose you will be as nothing and perish. Though you search for your enemies, you will not find them. Those who wage war against you will be as nothing at all. For I am the Lord your God who takes hold of your right hand and says to you, Do not fear; I will help you. Do not be afraid, you worm Jacob, little Israel, do not fear, for I myself will help you," declares the Lord, your Redeemer, the Holy One of Israel. "See, I will make you into a threshing sledge, new and sharp, with many teeth. You will thresh the mountains and crush them, and reduce the hills to chaff. You will winnow them,

the wind will pick them up, and a gale will blow them away. But you will rejoice in the Lord and glory in the Holy One of Israel."
— *Isaiah 41:9-16*

Fear not, for I have redeemed you; I have called you by name, you are mine. When you pass through the waters, I will be with you; and through the rivers, they shall not overwhelm you; when you walk through fire you shall not be burned, and the flame shall not consume you. For I am the Lord your God, the Holy One of Israel, your Savior.... Because you are precious in my eyes, and honored, and I love you.
— *Isaiah 43:1-4*

Look unto me, and be ye saved, all the ends of the earth, for I am God, and there is none else.
—*Isaiah 45:22*

Ah, Lord God! It is you who have made the heavens and the earth by your great power and by your outstretched arm! Nothing is too hard for you.
— *Jeremiah 32:17*

Thus says the Lord who made the earth, the Lord who formed it to establish it—the Lord is his name: Call to me and I will answer you, and will tell you great and hidden things that you have not known.
— *Jeremiah 33:2-3*

Steep your life in God-reality, God-initiative, God-provisions . . . You'll find all your everyday human concerns will be met.
— *Matthew 6:33*

Nothing will be impossible with God.
— *Luke 1:37*

And he said to them, "I saw Satan fall like lightning from heaven. Behold, I have given you authority to tread on serpents and scorpions, and over all the power of the enemy, and nothing shall hurt you.

Nevertheless, do not rejoice in this, that the spirits are subject to you, but rejoice that your names are written in heaven."
— *Luke 10:18-20*

We can be sure that every detail in our lives of love for God is worked into something good.
— *Romans 8:28*

Absolutely nothing can get between us and God's love.
— *Romans 8:39*

Be joyful in hope, patient in affliction, faithful in prayer.
— *Romans 12:12*

And do this, understanding the present time: The hour has already come for you to wake up from your slumber, because our salvation is nearer now than when we first believed. The night is nearly over; the day is almost here. So let us put aside the deeds of darkness and put on the armor of light.
— *Romans 13:11-12*

You are a God of hope; fill me with all joy and peace, as I trust in You, so that I may overflow with hope by the power of Your Holy Spirit
— *Romans 15:13*

For we walk by faith, not by sight.
— *2 Corinthians 5:7*

Though we walk in the flesh, we do not war according to the flesh, for the weapons of our warfare are not of the flesh, but divinely powerful for the destruction of fortresses. We are destroying speculations and every lofty thing raised up against the knowledge of God, and we are taking every thought captive to the obedience of Christ.
— *2 Corinthians 10:3-5*

Far above all rule and authority and power and dominion, and every name that is named, not only in this age, but also in the one to come.
— *Ephesians 1:21*

Put on the whole armor of God, that you may be able to stand against the wiles of the devil.
— *Ephesians 6:11*

For we wrestle not against flesh and blood, but against principalities, against powers, against the rulers of the darkness of this world, against spiritual wickedness in high places.
— *Ephesians 6:12*

Why take to you the whole armor of God, that you may be able to withstand in the evil day, and having done all, to stand.
— *Ephesians 6:13*

So that at the name of Jesus EVERY KNEE WILL BOW, of those who are in heaven and on earth and under the earth, and that every tongue will confess that Jesus Christ is Lord, to the glory of God the Father.
— *Philippians 2:10-11*

Submit yourselves, then, to God. Resist the devil, and he will flee from you. Come near to God and he will come near to you. Wash your hands, you sinners, and purify your hearts, you double-minded. Grieve, mourn and wail. Change your laughter to mourning and your joy to gloom. Humble yourselves before the Lord, and he will lift you up.
— *James 4:7-10*

You call out to God for help and he helps.
— *1 Peter 1:17*

Humble yourselves, therefore, under the mighty hand of God so that at the proper time he may exalt you, casting all your anxieties on him,

because he cares for you. Be sober-minded; be watchful. Your adversary the devil prowls around like a roaring lion, seeking someone to devour. Resist him, firm in your faith, knowing that the same kinds of suffering are being experienced by your brotherhood throughout the world.
— *1 Peter 5:6-9*

And there was war in heaven: Michael and his angels fought against the dragon; and the dragon fought and his angels. And the great dragon was cast out, that old serpent, called the Devil, and Satan, which deceives the whole world: he was cast out into the earth, and his angels were cast out with him.
— *Revelation 12:7-9*

These shall make war with the Lamb, and the Lamb shall overcome them: for he is Lord of lords, and King of kings: and they that are with him are called, and chosen, and faithful.
— *Revelation 17:14*

Chapter Ten

THOUGHTS

"The devil is not terribly frightened of our human efforts and credentials. But he knows his kingdom will be damaged when we begin to lift up our hearts to God."

— *Jim Cymbala*

Too low they build who build beneath the stars.
— *Edward Young*

Hoping is not dreaming . . . It means a confident, alert expectation that God will do what He said He will do.
— *Eugene H. Peterson*

We live by faith, we love by faith.
— *Beth Moore*

Christian discipleship is making a map of the faithfulness of God.
— *Eugene H. Peterson*

The beginning of anxiety is the end of faith, and the beginning of true faith is the end of anxiety.
— *George Müller*

I believe demoralization can occur when Satan figures out who you and I fear most that we are and what we fear we cannot do, then he sets out to confirm it. Can I get a testimony?
— *Beth Moore*

You will never learn faith in comfortable surroundings. God gives us the promises in a quiet hour; God seals our covenants with great and gracious words, then He steps back and waits to see how much we believe; then He lets the tempter come, and the test seems to contradict all that He has spoken. It is then that faith wins its crown. That is the time to lookup through the storm, and among the trembling, frightened seamen cry, "I believe God that it shall be even as it was told me."
— *Max Lucado*

Unless we are broken, we will never be touched by what breaks the heart of God.
— *Erwin Lutzer*

If Christ is not first with you, then Christ is nothing to you.
— *Charles Spurgeon*

I have learnt to love the darkness of sorrow; there you see the brightness of His face.
— *Madame Guyon*

With all my heart I believe that God is always good, always right and loves me in ways that I cannot comprehend.
— *Beth Moore*

God's mercies come day by day. They come when we need them — not earlier and not later. God gives us what we need today. If we needed more, He would give us more. When we need something else, He will give that as well. Nothing we truly need will ever be withheld from us. Search your problems, and within them you will discover the well-disguised mercies of God.
— *Dr. Ray Pritchard*

The instructed Christian whose faculties have been developed by the Word and the Spirit will not fear the devil. When necessary he will stand against the powers of darkness and overcome them by the blood of the Lamb and the word of his testimony. He will recognize the peril in which he lives and will know what to do about it, but he will practice the presence of God.
—*A.W. Tozer*

I fear John Knox's prayers more than an army of ten thousand men.
— *Mary, Queen of Scots*

To love at all is to be vulnerable. Love anything, and your heart will certainly be wrung and possibly be broken. If you want to make sure of keeping it intact, you must give your heart to no one, not even to an animal. Wrap it carefully round with hobbies and little luxuries; avoid all entanglements; lock it up safe in the casket or coffin of your selfishness.

But in that casket — safe, dark, motionless, airless — it will change. It will not be broken; it will become unbreakable, impenetrable, irredeemable.
— *C.S. Lewis*

When God gives you a vision and darkness follows, wait. God will bring the vision He has for you to reality in your life if you will wait on His timing. Never try to help God fulfill His word. Abram went through thirteen years of silence, but in those years all of his self-sufficiency was destroyed. He grew past the point of relying on his own common sense. Those years of silence were a time of discipline, not a period of God's displeasure. There is never any need to pretend that your life is filled with joy and confidence; just wait upon God and be grounded in Him *(see Isaiah 50:10-11)*.
— *Oswald Chambers*

Dear One, God doesn't just want us to defend ourselves in fierce seasons of battle. He wants us to wound the kingdom of darkness. I remember Keith and I watching one of the early Rocky sequels. We stared at the screen while Apollo Creed pummeled Rocky's poor face without getting a single return punch. Keith leaned over to me and said, "That's the old 'let 'em hit you in the face till they're tired' trick." Some of us think that if we just stand there and let Satan hit us long enough, he'll get tired. He's not getting tired! Hit him back, for crying out loud!
— *Beth Moore*

A stronghold is a mindset impregnated with hopelessness that causes me to accept as unchangeable something that we know is contrary to the will of God.
— *Jim Logan*

Delays are not refusals; many a prayer is registered, and underneath it the words: "My time is not yet come." God has a set time as well as a set purpose, and He who orders the bounds of our habitation orders also the time of our deliverance.
— *Unknown*

Sometimes life deals you a bad set of cards. What do you do then? You can get angry with God, or you can give up on God altogether. Or you can conclude that God doesn't know what he's doing. Or that the universe has spun out of control. Or you can choose to believe in God anyway. Often we mistake faith and our feelings. Faith isn't about my feelings, much less about my circumstances. Faith is a conscious choice I make, a moment by moment decision to believe that God is fully involved in my situation regardless of my current circumstances. Faith chooses to believe when it would be easier to stop believing.
— *Dr. Ray Pritchard, "Fire and Rain: The Wild-Hearted Faith of Elijah"*

Since we live in a world whose god is Satan, the possibility of being tempted, deceived and accused is continuous. If you allow his schemes to influence you, you can lose control to the degree that you have been deceived. If he can persuade you to believe a lie, he can control your life.
— *Dr. Neil T. Anderson*

God knows just when to withhold from us any visible sign of encouragement, and when to grant us such a sign. How good it is that we may trust Him anyway! When all visible evidences that He is remembering us are withheld, that is best; He wants us to realize that His Word, His promise of remembrance, is more substantial and dependable than any evidence of our senses. When He sends the visible evidence, that is well also; we appreciate it all the more after we have trusted Him without it. Those who are readiest to trust God without other evidence than His Word always receive the greatest number of visible evidences of His love.
— *C. G. Trumbull*

You were the victim of a terrible, ugly tragedy. But if you only see yourself as a rape victim for the rest of your life, you will never be free. You're a child of God. You can't fix the past, but you can be free from it. All of us have a number of hurtful, traumatic experiences in our past which have scarred us emotionally. You may have grown up with a physically, emotionally or sexually abusive parent. Any number

of traumatic, emotional events can clutter your soul with emotional baggage which seems to limit your maturity and block your freedom in Christ. You must renounce the experiences and lies that have controlled you and forgive those who have offended you.
— *Dr. Neil T. Anderson*

"If you think of this world as a place intended simply for our happiness, you find it quite intolerable: think of it as a place of training and correction and it's not so bad." We are ever the students. He is the teacher still. Trials rip away the flimsy fabric of self-sufficiency and become the raw material for God's miracles in our lives. And those miracles are a sudden glory. Someone once said, "Faith means believing in advance what will only make sense in reverse." Oh that we would trust Him even if the twists and turns never make sense this side of heaven. That's what trusting God is all about. As we live and move and have our being in Him, the dark places are simply opportunities to trust that He knows the way—and the perfect time to hold on tight.
— *C.S. Lewis*

I am a debtor to God's grace and forgiving mercy; but I am no debtor to His justice, for He will never accuse me of a debt already paid. Christ said, "It is finished!" and by that He meant, that whatever His people owed was wiped away forever from the book of remembrance.
— *Charles Spurgeon*

I have come to know a God who has a soft spot for rebels, who recruits people like the adulterer David, the whiner Jeremiah, the traitor Peter, and the human-rights abuser Saul of Tarsus. I have come to know a God whose Son made prodigals the heroes of his stories and the trophies of his ministry.
— *Philip Yancey*

The scriptural way to see things is to set the Lord always before us, put Christ in the center of our vision, and if Satan is lurking around he will appear on the margin only and be seen as but a shadow on the edge of the brightness. It is always wrong to reverse this – to set Satan in the focus of our vision and push God out to the margin. Nothing but tragedy can come of such inversion. The best way to keep the enemy out is to keep Christ in. The sheep need not be terrified by the wolf; they have but to stay close to the shepherd. It is not the praying sheep Satan fears, but the presence of the shepherd. The instructed Christian whose faculties have been developed by the Word and the Spirit will not fear the devil. When necessary he will stand against the powers of darkness and overcome them by the blood of the Lamb and the word of his testimony. He will recognize the peril in which he lives and will know what to do about it, but he will practice the presence of God and never allow himself to become devil-conscious.

—*A.W. Tozer*

Frodo: I can't do this, Sam.

Sam: I know. It's all wrong. By rights we shouldn't even be here. But we are. It's like in the great stories, Mr. Frodo. The ones that really mattered. Full of darkness and danger, they were. And sometimes you didn't want to know the end. Because how could the end be happy? How could the world go back to the way it was when so much bad had happened? But in the end, it's only a passing thing, this shadow. Even darkness must pass. A new day will come. And when the sun shines it will shine out the clearer. Those were the stories that stayed with you. That meant something, even if you were too small to understand why. But I think, Mr. Frodo, I do understand. I know now. Folk in those stories had lots of chances of turning back, only they didn't. They kept going. Because they were holding on to something.

Frodo: What are we holding onto, Sam?

Sam: That there's some good in this world, Mr. Frodo . . . and it's worth fighting for.

— *J.R.R. Tolkien, The Two Towers*

"Lie passive in God's hands, and know no will but His."

O child of suffering, be thou patient; God has not passed thee over in His providence. He who is the feeder of sparrows, will also furnish you with what you need. Sit not down in despair; hope on, hope ever. Take up the arms of faith against a sea of trouble, and your opposition shall yet end your distresses. There is One who careth for you. His eye is fixed on you, His heart beats with pity for your woe, and his hand omnipotent shall yet bring you the needed help. The darkest cloud shall scatter itself in showers of mercy. The blackest gloom shall give place to the morning. He, if thou art one of His family, will bind up thy wounds, and heal thy broken heart. Doubt not His grace because of thy tribulation, but believe that He loveth thee as much in seasons of trouble as in times of happiness. What a serene and quiet life might you lead if you would leave providing to the God of providence! With a little oil in the cruse, and a handful of meal in the barrel, Elijah outlived the famine, and you will do the same. If God cares for you, why need you care too? Can you trust Him for your soul, and not for your body? He has never refused to bear your burdens, He has never fainted under their weight. Come, then, soul! Have done with fretful care, and leave all thy concerns in the hand of a gracious God.

— *Charles Spurgeon*

Satan seeks to disgrace us, accuse us, and condemn us. We must daily set our faces like flint on the face of Christ and follow Him step by step to victory. Yes, you and I will still veer periodically from the path, no matter how obediently we want to walk. We are pilgrims with feet of clay. But no matter how long the detour has been, the return is only a shortcut away, because His light will always lead us right back to the path.

— *Beth Moore*

Suppose that the three Hebrew children had lost their faith and courage, and had complained, saying, "Why did not God keep us out of the furnace!" They would have been burned, and God would not have

been glorified. If there is a great trial in your life today, do not own it as a defeat, but continue, by faith, to claim the victory through Him who is able to make you more than a conqueror, and a glorious victory will soon be apparent. Let us learn that in all the hard places God brings us into, He is making opportunities for us to exercise such faith in Him as will bring about blessed results and greatly glorify His name.
— *Life of Praise*

Do you believe this? (John 11:26) Martha believed in the power available to Jesus Christ; she believed that if He had been there He could have healed her brother; she also believed that Jesus had a special intimacy with God, and that whatever He asked of God, God would do. But— she needed a closer personal intimacy with Jesus. Martha's theology had its fulfillment in the future. But Jesus continued to attract and draw her in until her belief became an intimate possession. It then slowly emerged into a personal inheritance —"Yes, Lord, I believe that You are the Christ . . ." *(John 11:27)*. Is the Lord dealing with you in the same way? Is Jesus teaching you to have a personal intimacy with Himself? Allow Him to drive His question home to you— "Do you believe this?" Are you facing an area of doubt in your life? Have you come, like Martha, to a crossroads of overwhelming circumstances where your theology is about to become a very personal belief? This happens only when a personal problem brings the awareness of our personal need. To believe is to commit. In the area of intellectual learning I commit myself mentally, and reject anything not related to that belief. In the realm of personal belief I commit myself morally to my convictions and refuse to compromise. But in intimate personal belief I commit myself spiritually to Jesus Christ and make a determination to be dominated by Him alone. Then, when I stand face to face with Jesus Christ and He says to me, "Do you believe this?" I find that faith is as natural as breathing. And I am staggered when I think how foolish I have been in not trusting Him earlier.
— *Oswald Chambers*

Evil never surrenders its hold without a sore fight. We never pass into any spiritual inheritance through the delightful exercises of a picnic, but always through the grim contentions of the battlefield. It is so in the secret realm of the soul. Every faculty which wins its spiritual freedom does so at the price of blood. Apollyon is not put to flight by a courteous request; he straddles across the full breadth of the way, and our progress has to be registered in blood and tears. This we must remember or we shall add to all the other burdens of life the gall of misinterpretation. We are not "born again" into soft and protected nurseries, but in the open country where we suck strength from the very terror of the tempest. "We must through much tribulation enter into the kingdom of God."

— *Dr. J. H. Jowett*

2 Kings 6:9
The iron did swim.

The axe-head seemed hopelessly lost, and as it was borrowed, the honour of the prophetic band was likely to be imperilled, and so the name of their God to be compromised. Contrary to all expectation, the iron was made to mount from the depth of the stream and to swim; for things impossible with man are possible with God. I knew a man in Christ but a few years ago who was called to undertake a work far exceeding his strength. It appeared so difficult as to involve absurdity in the bare idea of attempting it. Yet he was called thereto, and his faith rose with the occasion; God honoured his faith, unlooked for aid was sent, and the iron did swim. Another of the Lord's family was in grievous financial straits, he was able to meet all claims, and much more if he could have realized a certain portion of his estate, but he was overtaken with a sudden pressure; he sought for friends in vain, but faith led him to the unfailing Helper, and lo, the trouble was averted, his footsteps were enlarged, and the iron did swim. A third had a sorrowful case of depravity to deal with. He had taught, reproved, warned, invited, and interceded, but all in vain. Old Adam was too strong for young Melancthon, the stubborn spirit would not relent. Then came an agony of prayer, and before long a blessed answer was sent from heaven. The hard heart was broken, the iron did swim. Beloved reader, what is thy desperate case? What heavy matter hast thou in hand this evening? Bring it hither. The God of the prophets lives, and lives to help His saints. He will not suffer thee to lack any good thing. Believe thou in the Lord of hosts! Approach Him pleading the name of Jesus, and the iron shall swim; thou too shalt see the finger of God working marvels for His people. According to thy faith be it unto thee, and yet again the iron shall swim.

— *Charles Spurgeon*

1 Kings 12:24
This thing is from me.

"Life's disappointments are veiled love's appointments." — Rev. C. A. Fox

My child, I have a message for you today; let me whisper it in your ear, that it may gild with glory any storm clouds which may arise, and smooth the rough places upon which you may have to tread. It is short, only five words, but let them sink into your inmost soul; use them as a pillow upon which to rest your weary head. *This thing is from Me.* Have you ever thought of it, that all that concerns you concerns Me too? For, "he that toucheth you, toucheth the apple of mine eye" *(Zechariah 2:8)*. You are very precious in My sight *(Isaiah 43:4)*. Therefore, it is My special delight to educate you. I would have you learn when temptations assail you, and the "enemy comes in like a flood," that *this thing is from Me,* that your weakness needs My might, and your safety lies in letting Me fight for you. Are you in difficult circumstances, surrounded by people who do not understand you, who never consult your taste, who put you in the background? *This thing is from Me.* I am the God of circumstances. Thou camest not to thy place by accident, it is the very place God meant for thee. Have you not asked to be made humble? See then, I have placed you in the very school where this lesson is taught; your surroundings and companions are only working out My will. Are you in money difficulties? Is it hard to make both ends meet? *This thing is from Me,* for I am your purse-bearer and would have you draw from and depend upon Me. My supplies are limitless *(Philippians 4:19).* I would have you prove my promises. Let it not be said of you, "In this thing ye did not believe the Lord your God" *(Deuteronomy 1:32).* Are you passing through a night of sorrow? *This thing is from Me.* I am the Man of Sorrows and acquainted with grief. I have let earthly comforters fail you, that by turning to Me you may obtain everlasting consolation *(2 Thessalonians 2:16-17).* Have you longed to do some great work for Me and instead have been laid aside on a bed of pain and weakness? *This thing is from Me.* I could not get your attention in your busy days and I want to teach you some of my deepest lessons. "They also serve who only stand and wait." Some of My greatest workers are those shut out from active service, that they may learn to wield the weapon of all — prayer. This day I place in your hand this pot of holy oil. Make use of it free, my child. Let every circumstance that arises, every word that pains you, every interruption that would make you impatient, every revelation of your weakness be anointed with it. The sting will go as you learn to see Me in all things.

— *Laura A. Barter Snow*

Hebrews 12:2
Looking unto Jesus.

It is ever the Holy Spirit's work to turn our eyes away from self to Jesus; but Satan's work is just the opposite of this, for he is constantly trying to make us regard ourselves instead of Christ. He insinuates, "Your sins are too great for pardon; you have no faith; you do not repent enough; you will never be able to continue to the end; you have not the joy of His children; you have such a wavering hold of Jesus." All these are thoughts about self, and we shall never find comfort or assurance by looking within. But the Holy Spirit turns our eyes entirely away from self: He tells us that we are nothing, but that "Christ is all in all." Remember, therefore, it is not thy hold of Christ that saves thee — it is Christ; it is not thy joy in Christ that saves thee — it is Christ; it is not even faith in Christ, though that be the instrument — it is Christ's blood and merits; therefore, look not so much to thy hand with which thou art grasping Christ, as to Christ; look not to thy hope, but to Jesus, the source of thy hope; look not to thy faith, but to Jesus, the author and finisher of thy faith. We shall never find happiness by looking at our prayers, our doings, or our feelings; it is what Jesus is, not what we are, that gives rest to the soul. If we would at once overcome Satan and have peace with God, it must be by "looking unto Jesus." Keep thine eye simply on Him; let His death, His sufferings, His merits, His glories, His intercession, be fresh upon thy mind; when thou wakest in the morning look to Him; when thou liest down at night look to Him. Oh! let not thy hopes or fears come between thee and Jesus; follow hard after Him, and He will never fail thee.

— *Charles Spurgeon*

Song of Solomon 1:7
Tell me . . . where Thou feedest, where Thou makest Thy flock to rest at noon.

These words express the desire of the believer after Christ, and his longing for present communion with Him. Where doest Thou feed Thy flock? In Thy house? I will go, if I may find Thee there. In private prayer? Then I will pray without ceasing. In the Word? Then I will read it diligently. In Thine ordinances? Then I will walk in them with all my heart. Tell me where Thou feedest, for wherever Thou standest as the Shepherd, there will I lie down as a sheep; for none but Thyself can supply my need. I cannot be satisfied to be apart from Thee. My soul hungers and thirsts for the refreshment of Thy presence. "Where dost Thou make Thy flock to rest at noon?" for whether at dawn or at noon, my only rest must be where Thou art and Thy beloved flock. My soul's rest must be a grace-given rest, and can only be found in Thee. Where is the shadow of that rock? Why should I not repose beneath it? "Why should I be as one that turneth aside by the flocks of thy companions?" Thou hast companions — why should I not be one? Satan tells me I am unworthy; but I always was unworthy, and yet Thou hast long loved me; and therefore my unworthiness cannot be a bar to my having fellowship with Thee now. It is true I am weak in faith, and prone to fall, but my very feebleness is the reason why I should always be where

Thou feedest Thy flock, that I may be strengthened, and preserved in safety beside the still waters. Why should I turn aside? There is no reason why I should, but there are a thousand reasons why I should not, for Jesus beckons me to come. If He withdrew Himself a little, it is but to make me prize His presence more. Now that I am grieved and distressed at being away from Him, He will lead me yet again to that sheltered nook where the lambs of His fold are sheltered from the burning sun.

— *Charles Spurgeon*

Joshua 1:2
The land which I do give them, even the children of Israel.

Believing Before Seeing — God here speaks in the immediate present. It is not something He is going to do, but something He does do, this moment. So faith ever speaks. So God ever gives. So He is meeting you today, in the present moment. This is the test of faith. So long as you are waiting for a thing, hoping for it, looking for it, you are not believing. It may be hope, it may be earnest desire, but it is not faith; for "faith is the substance of things hoped for, the evidence of things not seen." The command in regard to believing prayer is the present tense. "When ye pray, believe that ye receive the things that ye desire, and ye shall have them." Have we come to that moment? Have we met God in His everlasting NOW?

— *Taken from "Christ in the book of Joshua" by A.B. Simpson*

True faith counts on God, and believes before it sees. Naturally, we want some evidence that our petition is granted before we believe; but when we walk by faith we need no other evidence than God's Word. He has spoken, and according to our faith it shall be done unto us. We shall see because we have believed, and this faith sustains us in the most trying places, when everything around us seems to contradict God's Word. The Psalmist says, "I had fainted, unless I had believed to see the goodness of the Lord in the land of living" *(Psalm 27:13)*. He did not see as yet the Lord's answer to his prayers, but he believed to see; and this kept him from fainting. If we have

the faith that believes to see, it will keep us from growing discouraged. We shall "laugh at impossibilities," we shall watch with delight to see how God is going to open up a path through the Red Sea when there is no human way out of our difficulty. It is just in such places of severe testing that our faith grows and strengthens. Have you been waiting upon God, dear troubled one, during long nights and weary days, and have feared that you were forgotten? Nay, lift up your head, and begin to praise Him even now for the deliverance which is on its way to you.
—*Life of Praise*

We become saints at the moment of salvation and live as saints in our daily experience as we continue to believe what God has done and as we continue to affirm who we really are in Christ. If you fail to see yourself as a child of God, you will struggle vainly to live like one, and Satan will have little trouble convincing you that you are no different from who you were before Christ and that you have no value to God or anyone else. But appropriating by faith the radical transformation of your core identity from sinner to saint will have a powerful, positive effect on your daily resistance to sin and Satan.
— *Dr. Neil T. Anderson*

Psalm 43:5
Why art thou cast down, O my soul.

Is there ever any ground to be cast down? There are two reasons, but only two. If we are as yet unconverted, we have ground to be cast down; or if we have been converted and live in sin, then we are rightly cast down. But except for these two things there is no ground to be cast down, for all else may be brought before God in prayer with supplication and thanksgiving. And regarding all our necessities, all our difficulties, all our trials, we may exercise faith in the power of God, and in the love of God. "Hope thou in God." Oh, remember this: There is never a time when we may not hope in God. Whatever our necessities, however great our difficulties, and though to all appearance help is impossible, yet our business is to hope in God, and it will be found that it is not in

vain. In the Lord's own time help will come. Oh, the hundreds, yea, the thousands of times that I have found it thus within the past seventy years and four months! When it seemed impossible that help could come, help did come; for God has His own resources. He is not confined. In ten thousand different ways, and at ten thousand different times God may help us. Our business is to spread our cases before the Lord, in childlike simplicity to pour out all our heart before God, saying, "I do not deserve that Thou shouldst hear me and answer my requests, but for the sake of my precious Lord Jesus; for His sake answer my prayer, and give me grace quietly to wait till it please Thee to answer my prayer. For I believe Thou wilt do it in Thine own time and way." "For I shall yet praise him." More prayer, more exercise of faith, more patient waiting, and the result will be blessing, abundant blessing. Thus I have found it many hundreds of times, and therefore I continually say to myself, "Hope thou in God."
—*George Müller*

Luke 1:38
Behold, the bondslave of the Lord; be it done to me according to your word.

Nothing Is Impossible With God — If God wants something done, can it be done? In other words, if God has a goal for your life, can it be blocked, or is its fulfillment uncertain or impossible? I am personally convinced that no goal God has for my life is impossible or uncertain, nor can it be blocked. Imagine God saying, "I've called you into existence, I've made you My child, and I have something for you to do. I know you won't be able to do it, but give it your best shot." That's ludicrous! It's like saying to your child, "I want to you to mow the lawn. Unfortunately, the lawn is full of rocks, the mower doesn't work, and there's no gas. But give it your best shot." Even secular scholars say that issuing a command that cannot be obeyed will undermine authority. God had a staggering goal for a little maiden named Mary. An angel told her that she would bear a son while still a virgin, and that her son would be the Savior of the world. When she inquired about this seemingly impossible feat, the angel simply said, "Nothing will be impossible with God" *(Luke 1:37)*. You wouldn't give your child a task he couldn't complete, and God doesn't assign to you goals you can't achieve. His goals for you are possible, certain and achievable. When God's will for us appears impossible, let's say with Mary: "Behold, the bondslave of the Lord; be it done to me according to your word" *(Luke 1:38)*. Imagine the overwhelming assignment that confronted Mary. She was to have a baby without being with a man. She was to raise the child who would save the world. The entire course of history would be altered, and the eternal destiny of believers would be changed. The fact that you are celebrating Christmas today is proof that Mary's child Jesus was indeed the world-changing Son of God. Despite the staggering nature of the task announced by the angel, Mary gave herself to accomplish God's will. God is still looking for a few bondslaves who will dare to believe that nothing is impossible with God. Prayer: Lord, I yield to You as Your bondslave. I choose to believe that whatever You want me to do I can do.

— *Dr. Neil T. Anderson*

Psalm 27:14
"Wait on the Lord."

It may seem an easy thing to wait, but it is one of the postures which a Christian soldier learns not without years of teaching. Marching and quick-marching are much easier to God's warriors than standing still. There are hours of perplexity when the most willing spirit, anxiously desirous to serve the Lord, knows not what part to take. Then what shall it do? Vex itself by despair? Fly back in cowardice, turn to the right hand in fear, or rush forward in presumption? No, but simply wait. Wait in prayer, however. Call upon God, and spread the case before him; tell him your difficulty, and plead his promise of aid. In dilemmas between one duty and another, it is sweet to be humble as a child, and wait with simplicity of soul upon the Lord. It is sure to be well with us when we feel and know our own folly, and are heartily willing to be guided by the will of God. But wait in faith. Express your unstaggering confidence in him; for unfaithful, untrusting waiting, is but an insult to the Lord. Believe that if he keep you tarrying even till midnight, yet he will come

at the right time; the vision shall come and shall not tarry. Wait in quiet patience, not rebelling because you are under the affliction, but blessing your God for it. Never murmur against the second cause, as the children of Israel did against Moses; never wish you could go back to the world again, but accept the case as it is, and put it as it stands, simply and with your whole heart, without any self-will, into the hand of your covenant God, saying, "Now, Lord, not my will, but thine be done. I know not what to do; I am brought to extremities, but I will wait until thou shalt cleave the floods, or drive back my foes. I will wait, if thou keep me many a day, for my heart is fixed upon thee alone, O God, and my spirit waiteth for thee in the full conviction that thou wilt yet be my joy and my salvation, my refuge and my strong tower."
— *Charles Spurgeon*

1 Peter 5:7
Cast all your anxiety on Him because He cares for you.

Let's assume you have sought God's will for a certain direction, and you believe that He has led you to make specific plans. The problem is you are still worried about whether your plans will come about as you have hoped. When I'm facing such situations, I try to follow the six steps described below to limit my anxious feelings. *First* — state the problem. A problem well stated is half solved. In anxious states of mind, people can't see the forest for the trees. Put the problem in perspective. Will it matter for eternity? The danger at this juncture is to seek ungodly counsel. The world is glutted with magicians and sorcerers who will promise incredible results. Their appearance may be striking. Their personality may be charming. But they are bankrupt of character. Avoid them *(Psalm 1:1)*. *Second* — separate the facts from the assumptions. Since we don't know what's going to happen tomorrow, we make assumptions, and we usually assume the worst. If the assumption is accepted as truth, it will drive your mind to its anxiety limits. Therefore, you must separate assumptions from facts. *Third* — determine what you have the right or ability to control. You are responsible for that which you can control, and you are not responsible for that which you can't. Don't try to cast

your responsibility onto Christ; He will throw it back. *Fourth* — list everything you can do which is related to the situation that is under your responsibility. When people don't assume their responsibility, they turn to temporary cures for their anxiety, like eating, TV, sex or drugs. *Fifth* — once you are sure you have fulfilled your responsibility, see if there is any way you can help others. Turning your attention away from your own self-absorption and onto helping people around you is not only the loving thing to do, but it also brings a special inner peace. *Sixth* — the rest is God's responsibility, except for your prayer, according to Philippians 4:6-8. So assume your responsibility, but cast your anxiety on Christ. Prayer: Lord, help me recognize the difference between today's responsibilities and anxieties, then put them in their proper places.
— *Dr. Neil T. Anderson*

Isaiah 49:16
Behold, I have graven thee upon the palms of my hands.

No doubt a part of the wonder which is concentrated in the word "Behold," is excited by the unbelieving lamentation of the preceding sentence. Zion said, "The Lord hath forsaken me, and my God hath forgotten me." How amazed the divine mind seems to be at this wicked unbelief! What can be more astounding than the unfounded doubts and fears of God's favoured people? The Lord's loving word of rebuke should make us blush; He cries, "How can I have forgotten thee, when I have graven thee upon the palms of my hands? How darest thou doubt my constant remembrance, when the memorial is set upon my very flesh?" O unbelief, how strange a marvel thou art! We know not which most to wonder at, the faithfulness of God or the unbelief of His people. He keeps His promise a thousand times, and yet the next trial makes us doubt Him. He never faileth; He is never a dry well; He is never as a setting sun, a passing meteor, or a melting vapour; and yet we are as continually vexed with anxieties, molested with suspicions, and disturbed with fears, as if our God were the mirage of the desert. "Behold," is a word intended to excite admiration. Here, indeed, we have a theme for marvelling. Heaven and earth may well be astonished that rebels should obtain so great a nearness to the heart of infinite love as to be written upon the palms of His hands. "I have graven thee." It does not say, "Thy name." The name is there, but that is not all: "I have graven thee." See the fullness of this! I have graven thy person, thine image, thy case, thy circumstances, thy sins, thy temptations, thy weaknesses, thy wants, thy works; I have graven thee, everything about thee, all that concerns thee; I have put thee altogether there. Wilt thou ever say again that thy God hath forsaken thee when He has graven thee upon His own palms?

— *Charles Spurgeon*

Mark 15:34

And at three in the afternoon Jesus cried out in a loud voice, "Eloi, Eloi, lema sabachthani?" (which means "My God, my God, why have you forsaken me?")

The following comes from a Chinese house church pastor who had been arrested and held for three weeks. He says his experience was "going with Christ to the Garden and to the Cross."

But it is not all triumph. I know some pastors who said they just smiled all the time from the moment they were arrested, and felt unutterable joy the whole time. I suppose that is possible. After all, Shadrach, Meshach and Abednego seemed to be very calm throughout their ordeal. But we must not make that the test of true spirituality. The Psalmists are full of despair and questioning as they go through hard times. So were Jeremiah and Job and Habakkuk. And most sobering of all, our Lord Himself was heard to cry from the Cross, "My God, my God, why have you forsaken me?" *(Mark 15:34)* This is the dark side of the experience. What makes suffering hardest to bear are the questions, the voices that well up within each of us, that are full of doubts, despair and depression. And I believe this is OK. As humans we were not meant to suffer. We were made to be part of a perfect world, with no sorrow or sighing, an Eden where everyone was righteous and fulfilled. So when we suffer, there is a sense in which our bodies and spirits witness saying, "This is unnatural, this is not why we were created." In my own case, I wondered whether God had turned His back on me, or was punishing me for past sins. But most of these doubts were not weaknesses as such; they were attempts to comprehend the incomprehensible. Where is God here? What's He up to? How can this possibly extend His kingdom? How is His glory served by one of my sisters being raped by an interrogator? The fact is, when we suffer, there is so much that we cannot understand. I read somewhere that "because we are human, we yearn to understand, but because we are human, we cannot understand." Suffering puts us in our place. It humbles us to realize that we are not really in charge of our lives. This is a hard realization. God is in charge, and His purposes can be hard to discern at times. He takes even the sin of the world, and turns it to good account. We often do not see how He does this, but we believe it. Accepting it in faith is never easy when you are suffering.

— *Rev. Paul Estabrooks*

Colossians 2:6
As you therefore have received Christ Jesus the Lord, so walk in Him.

There are three ways of responding to the demonic taunts and barbs being thrown at you during your daily walk with Christ, and two of these ways are wrong. First, the most defeated people are those who consider demonic thoughts and believe them. A subtle thought is shot into your mind: "You don't pray, read your Bible, or witness like you should. How could God love you?" That's a bald-faced lie because God's love is unconditional. But you start thinking about your failures and agreeing that you're probably not very lovable to God. Pretty soon you're sitting in the middle of the street going nowhere. These Christians are totally defeated simply because they have been duped into believing that God doesn't love them, or that they will never be a victorious Christian, or that they are a helpless victim of the past. There is no reason why they can't get up immediately and start walking again, but they have believed a lie and the lie controls their life. The second response is just as unproductive. You try to argue with the demons: "I am not ugly or stupid. I am a victorious Christian." You're proud that you don't believe what they say, but they're still controlling you and setting your agenda. You're standing in the middle of the street shouting at them when you should be marching forward. We are not to believe evil spirits, nor are we to dialogue with them. Instead, we are to ignore them and choose the truth. You're equipped with the armor of God; they can't touch you unless you drop your guard. With every arrow of temptation, accusation or deception they shoot at you, simply raise the shield of faith, deflect the attack, and walk on. Take every thought captive to the obedience of Christ. The way to defeat the lie is by choosing the truth.

— *Dr. Neil T. Anderson*

1 Corinthians 2:7-8
We declare God's wisdom, a mystery that has been hidden and that God destined for our glory before time began. None of the rulers of this age understood it, for if they had, they would not have crucified the Lord of glory.

Have you ever noticed the strategy Satan used throughout Old Testament history? His attacks were aimed at preventing the birth of the Messiah at Bethlehem, but, once Jesus was born, Satan's tactics changed somewhat. In some instances, he tried to kill Jesus before the Lord could reach the cross. At other times, Satan engineered numerous attempts to discredit Him—to cause Him to stumble or to sin. But Satan met defeat at the cross. He failed to understand God's strategy, and his final blunder actually forced events so that Jesus, though innocent, was condemned to die. The Apostle Paul noted that Satan did not understand this in 1 Corinthians 2:8. Since that time, Satan's tactics have changed. He's still concerned about preventing the Word—the Word that was with God and is God *(John 1:1)*—from reaching people who are under Satan's dominion. His attack is now two-pronged. First Satan concentrates on the life and name of Jesus which each and every believer bears as the Lord's representative. I believe it is important for Christians undergoing persecution to realize the attack they are under is actually directed not at them, but at the life of Jesus in them, a life which they have power to transmit to others. Satan will make every effort to discredit you, to frighten you and to silence your witness in order that the new life in you stops with you. Sometimes Satan overreaches himself, just as he did at the cross, and sends a believer to a martyr's grave but that life lives on in other believers who continue to bear witness more gloriously and triumphantly than ever.

— *Brother Andrew*

Christ is building His kingdom with earth's broken things. Men want only the strong, the successful, the victorious, the unbroken, in building their kingdoms; but God is the God of the unsuccessful, of those who have failed. Heaven is filling with earth's broken lives, and there is no bruised reed that Christ cannot take and restore to glorious blessedness and beauty. He can take the life crushed by pain or sorrow and make it into a harp whose music shall be all praise. He can lift earth's saddest failure up to heaven's glory.

—*J. R. Miller*

Jeremiah 29:11
"For I know the plans that I have for you," declares the LORD, "plans for welfare and not for calamity to give you a future and a hope."

I believe that God desires all His children to be successful, significant, fulfilled, satisfied, joyful, secure, and to live in peace. From birth you have been developing in your mind a means for experiencing these values and reaching other goals in life. Consciously or subconsciously you continue to formulate and adjust your plans for achieving these goals. But sometimes your well-intended plans and noble-sounding goals are not completely in harmony with God's plans and goals for you. "How can I know if what I believe is right?" you may be wondering. "Must I wait until I am 45 years old or until I experience some kind of mid-life crisis to discover that what I believed was wrong?" I don't think so. I believe that God has designed us in such a way that we can know on a regular basis if our belief system is properly aligned with God's truth. God has established a feedback system which is designed to grab your attention so you can examine the validity of your goal. That system is your emotions. When an experience or relationship leaves you feeling angry, anxious or depressed, those emotional signposts are there to alert you that you may be cherishing a faulty goal which is based on a wrong belief. If our goals are blocked, we become angry. If our goals are uncertain, we feel anxious. If we perceive our goals as impossible, we become depressed because the heart of depression is hopelessness. Can any God-given goal be blocked, uncertain or impossible? Put another way, if God wants something done, can it be done? Of course! The question is do we have a biblical understanding of success, significance, fulfillment, satisfaction, joy, security and peace? When we see and pursue these values from God's perspective, we will reach our goals because they are God's goals for us.

— *Dr. Neil T. Anderson*

Romans 8:1
There is no condemnation.

Many years ago when our boys were very young, we spent hours teaching them how to play baseball. It is amazing to go watch little kids play ball. You see kids at bat and the ball comes six feet over their head and they're swinging at it. Then a ball comes right down the middle and they just stand there. The coach says "Stay!" and they start running. The coach says "Run!" and they stay put. I remember one game where the coach told one of the outfielders, "Move up, come on, move up." The kid didn't want to. So the coach moved him up. You could just see the terror on his face. And Babe Ruth is at the plate. He takes this mighty swing and BOOM! there goes the ball. The outfielder is petrified! He can't move and the ball goes right through his legs. The tears well up in his eyes and he's trying to blink them back. The coach who moved him up said, "That's all right! That's OK! Nice try!" What do you mean nice try? He didn't even move a muscle! But at least it didn't hit him in the face. "Nice try. You'll catch it next time!" A shy, half-grin spreads across his face, as if to say, "Yeah, I did pretty good, didn't I?" That's what God does when we fail. He helps us back up, he tells us where we went wrong, and he puts us back in the game. That's what Paul means when he says there is no condemnation for those who are in Jesus Christ. Some Christians go through life with a heavy load of guilt not just because they struggle but because they feel condemned by God. They feel like God hates them. But he doesn't. His thoughts toward us are thoughts of love. Even when he must discipline us severely, he does it for our own good. Even his chastising is for our ultimate benefit. I don't know of any truth more important, more satisfying, or more liberating than the great truth that for those who know Jesus Christ, there is no condemnation.

Why? Because Jesus paid it all.
Why? Because your sins are gone.
Why? Because Jesus condemned sin by his death on the cross.

If he condemned sin by his death on the cross, God will never condemn you.
The devil condemns us day and night and whispers in our ear, "Condemned! Condemned!"
God says, "No condemnation!"
Who are you going to believe? The devil or God?
You'll have to make up your own mind, but I'm going to believe what God has said.

I urge you with all of my heart, with every fiber of my being, if you are not sure, if you do not know where you stand, run to Jesus Christ and embrace the cross. If you are outside of Christ, come by faith to Jesus. When you come, you will discover the most liberating truth in the world—that in Christ there is no condemnation.
— *Dr. Ray Pritchard*

PRAYER JOURNAL   *Date Answered*

_____   _____

_____   _____

_____   _____

_____   _____

_____   _____

_____   _____

_____   _____

_____   _____

_____   _____

_____   _____

_____   _____

_____   _____

_____   _____

_____   _____

_____   _____

_____   _____

_____   _____

_____   _____

_____   _____

_____   _____

_____   _____

PRAYER JOURNAL   *Date Answered*

_____ _____

_____ _____

_____ _____

_____ _____

_____ _____

_____ _____

_____ _____

_____ _____

_____ _____

_____ _____

_____ _____

_____ _____

_____ _____

_____ _____

_____ _____

_____ _____

_____ _____

_____ _____

_____ _____

_____ _____

PRAYER JOURNAL   *Date Answered*

_____   _____

_____   _____

_____   _____

_____   _____

_____   _____

_____   _____

_____   _____

_____   _____

_____   _____

_____   _____

_____   _____

_____   _____

_____   _____

_____   _____

_____   _____

_____   _____

_____   _____

_____   _____

PRAYER JOURNAL

PRAYER JOURNAL   *Date Answered*

_____   _____

_____   _____

_____   _____

_____   _____

_____   _____

_____   _____

_____   _____

_____   _____

_____   _____

_____   _____

_____   _____

_____   _____

_____   _____

_____   _____

_____   _____

_____   _____

_____   _____

_____   _____

_____   _____

_____   _____

MY PRAYER FOR YOU:

Heavenly Father, your warriors are
preparing for battle. Please give them the strength,
the endurance, and the wisdom they need
to wage war as they lay hold of the victory
that is already theirs in Christ.
I ask this in the precious
name of Jesus,
Amen.

Be wise. Be strong. Be fearless. Be God's.

I'd love to hear from you.
Please feel free to contact me at
www.KathrynMcBride.com.

Letcetera
PUBLISHING
CHICAGO

www.letceterapublishing.com

Made in United States
Orlando, FL
14 November 2022

24528144R00124